Wealth & Wellbeing

A *comprehensive Guide to* **Investments & Retirement Planning**

With examples & spread-sheets

Inder Kumar Achplani

www.whitefalconpublishing.com

Wealth & Wellbeing
Inder Kumar Achplani

www.whitefalconpublishing.com

All rights reserved
First Edition, 2022
© Inder Kumar Achplani, 2022
Cover design by White Falcon Publishing, 2022
Cover image source freepik.com

No part of this publication may be reproduced, or stored in a retrieval system, or transmitted in any form by means of electronic, mechanical, photocopying or otherwise, without prior written permission from the author.

The contents of this book have been certified and timestamped on the POA Network blockchain as a permanent proof of existence. Scan the QR code or visit the URL given on the back cover to verify the blockchain certification for this book.

The views expressed in this work are solely those of the author and do not reflect the views of the publisher, and the publisher hereby disclaims any responsibility for them.

Requests for permission should be addressed to
achpalani@gmail.com

ISBN - 978-1-63640-609-1

In loving memory of

Late Shri Krishan Kumar Achplani
(Sep.1954 – Apr.2021)

My first investment guru who taught me the
'Value of money'
&
Paved way for my 'wealth creation'

Dedication

This book is affectionately
Dedicated to our beloved
Kunal

Love you beta!!!

My Sincere Thanks

To

Mr. Pramod K Chokhani,
B.Com (Gold Medalist)
Chartered Accountant & Cost Accountant

Ms. Tanya Chokhani,
Chartered Accountant & Company Secretary

&

Ms. Ritika Ahuja
Masters in Economics
(Gold Medalist)

PREFACE

It is my strong belief that everyone can become a multi-millionaire if not a billionaire. The only thing required is the will to become wealthy as 'wealth creation is a mindset. Steps to wealth creation have been explained in this book. Although we have been advised time and again to save money but the difference between savings and investments is neither taught to us in school/college nor by anyone other in a structured manner. Whatever we learn about investments is generally hear-say and advised by friends/colleagues/agents/advisors or websites. Although they may be giving you correct advice but confined only to the product or products they are aware of or dealing with in the case of advisors/agents/websites.

In this book, I endeavor to discuss each option available for investing our hard-earned money along with the pros-n-cons of each investment option and even prioritize the available options depending upon our time horizon, financial goals/objectives, aspirations, expectations, etc.

It is a fact that everybody is worried about their life expectancy and therefore most of us take Life Insurance and try to cover ourselves and our families and also for medical exigencies as a medical treatment has gone very costly in our country nowadays. However, the dilemma is how much is sufficient? Unfortunately, we are not so much particular with the insurance of our property and are even not aware of personal accident cover which can come in handy in the hour of need. This book explains each insurance option available and tries to answer your queries about how much is sufficient, be it life insurance, medical insurance, top-up and super top-up medical policies, property insurance, personal accident cover, etc.

One of the inspirations for writing this book is a quote from investment banker Mr. Warren Buffet "put your money to work, otherwise, you have to work until you die". This book explains what is required to ensure a 'healthy, wealthy and peaceful' retired life by not only explaining the available investment options e.g. EPF, PPF, NPS, SCSS, MIS, GOI Bonds, FDs, KVP, NSC, etc. to ensure financially sound 'second innings' of life but they are explained by way of examples and spread-sheets.

In the illustrations, I have tried to take samples of all sections of society i.e. persons who are having limited retirement corpus, persons with liabilities on their heads even after retirement, and also persons who have built healthy 'retirement corpus' and are now in a fix where to invest their life-long savings safely, securely and also earn better returns. The difference between "Will" & "Nomination" is also discussed in the book.

Many people are scared of numbers and calculations when it comes to tax planning or filing of IT Returns although they have been made very simple and easy by the Government. Moreover, there are many legal ways to save taxes and each such option is discussed in this book.

As my endeavor through this book is not only to make you wealthy but also to ensure your well-being, "will & nomination", 'Retirement Satisfaction Guide' and 'steps to choose happiness' also have been explained in the book.

I am sure that this book will not only help you in your journey of "Wealth Creation" but also pave way for your Healthy, Wealthy, and Prosperous Life.

Best of Luck!

Inder Kumar Achplani

CONTENTS

1. INTRODUCTION 1
2. BASICS OF INVESTMENT 4
3. WEALTH CREATION 6
4. INSURANCE 10
   - 4.1 LIFE INSURANCE 11
   - 4.2 MEDICAL INSURANCE 13
   - 4.3 PERSONAL ACCIDENT COVER 16
   - 4.4 PROPERTY INSURANCE 17
5. INFLATION 18
6. POWER OF COMPOUNDING 23
7. INVESTMENT PLANNING 26
8. CONTINGENCY FUNDS 30
9. ASSET ALLOCATION 34
10. OBTAIN PAN CARD 36
11. TAX DEDUCTIONS 39
12. FILING OF INCOME TAX RETURNS 43
13. PUBLIC PROVIDENT FUND 51
14. NATIONAL PENSION SCHEME 57
15. POST OFFICE SCHEMES 66
    - 15.1 KISAN VIKAS PATRA (KVP) 67
    - 15.2 NATIONAL SAVINGS CERTIFICATE (NSC) 69
    - 15.3 SUKANYA SAMRIDHI SCHEME 70
    - 15.4 MONTHLY INCOME SCHEME ACCOUNT (MIS) 72
    - 15.5 TIME DEPOSIT ACCOUNT (TD) 74
16. SENIOR CITIZEN SAVINGS SCHEME 76
17. PRADHAN MANTRI VAYA VANDANA YOJANA 79

18. DEPOSIT INSURANCE & CREDIT GUARANTE CORPORATION 82
19. FIXED DEPOSITS 85
20. COMPANY FIXED DEPOSITS 88
21. FLOATING RATE SAVINGS BONDS (TAXABLE) – 2020 91
22. MUTUAL FUNDS 93
23. INVESTMENT IN EQUITY SHARES 104
24. INVESTMENT IN GOLD 110
25. INVESTMENT IN REAL ESTATE 114
26. CIBIL SCORE 121
27. LOAN AGAINST SECURITIES 125
28. REVERSE MORTGAGE 128
29. RETIREMENT PLANNING 133
30. FINANCIAL PLANNING FOR SENIOR CITIZENS 147
31. STEPS TO RETIREMENT PLANNING & ILLUSTRATIONS 150
32. RETIREMENT SATISFACTION GUIDE 197
33. WILL AND NOMINATION 201
34. STEPS TO CHOOSE HAPPINESS 205

"Know what you own, and know why you own it."

-Peter Lynch

Do your homework before making a decision. Once you've made a decision, make sure to re-evaluate your portfolio on a timely basis. A wise holding today may not be a wise holding in the future.

1.
INTRODUCTION

From the time you start your professional journey, you dream of becoming a "Millionaire" and I strongly feel you should always "**dream big**" to achieve big but the journey of becoming a millionaire will always be full of challenges and the most crucial part of this journey will be your '**first step**'. Resolve to take first step and start your journey to become multi-millionaire.

Rich and Wealthy are generally used as synonyms. However, they are two different words although very difficult to spot the differences. Being rich means having a lot of money or income. It comes down to how much you have at your disposal i.e. it may be due to inheritance, your income, etc. but it may also be through the large debt you have taken for maintaining rich and famous life style e.g. palatial house, big cars, designer jewelry, costly dresses, etc. Needless to give examples by name of many such rich people who were maintaining the 'richy-rich' lifestyle and are now absconding as they were unable to re-pay the loans they had taken. Instead, a wealthy person saves as much money as possible and invests it in assets.

Being wealthy is not only having enough money to meet your needs but it's about amassing assets and making your money work for you i.e. it's having a significant '**net worth**'.

Net worth in simple terms is the figure you get when you add up everything you own from the value of your home, car, furniture/fixture, etc. to the cash in your bank accounts and then subtracting from that all you have to re-pay as your debts e.g. house loan, car loan, even credit card balances, etc. In financial terms what you own is called '**assets**' and what you owe is called '**liabilities**'.

Theoretically, net worth is the value in 'cash' you would have if you sell everything you own and paid off all your debts. This number may be negative when you start your professional journey as you may take a loan for buying a flat and/or a car, etc. No worries, material comforts are also necessary to make you 'happy' but this remains to be seen how much money can make you happy?

It is often said that money can buy anything but 'happiness' because happiness is internal. However, you must first meet your basic needs to attain that happiness. It reminded me of Maslow's theory of needs. Maslow discussed the hierarchy of needs starting from the most basic need for physical survival and this is the first thing that motivates our behavior. Once that level is fulfilled the next level is up that motivates us, and so on.

We are on our journey to become wealthy yet we have to take care of at least the basic needs not only for ourselves but for our families too. Being wealthy doesn't mean you live like a miser but you have to learn to respect the money.

I have read about many Indians who started their journey from scratch and reached the sky. In fact, in my professional journey of almost four decades, I have personally met many such people becoming "rags to riches" and few of them influenced my journey to become wealthy. I listened to their stories, their hard work, dedication, dreams, and how they fulfilled them which impressed me a lot.

I may not be wrong if I say that they are my inspiration to write this book because I strongly feel 'if there is a will, there is a way". It will be up to you to decide your goal and this book will guide you to reach there.

In my book on "Decision Making", I have described the essentials of decision making. Decision-making is the art of selecting the best alternative out of many alternatives available. Selection of a particular alternative from the various choices available requires 'courage" and courage comes from 'confidence'. However, to be convinced of your choice, you require 'competence' on the subject where you are taking the decision. Last but not the least, it requires 'commitment' i.e. will to make a decision and stick to it.

In the decision making process, it works in reverse order i.e. you decide to become **'wealthy'** therefore be **committed** to your decision as this journey will be full of challenges and there will be times when you will look for momentary pleasures and may sacrifice your goals if you are not committed.

The next most important is your **competence** in this domain. Many of us know many things about investments but most of them are hear-say as we were never taught about investments in our school/colleges. If we invest on the advice of our Agents, they may give us the right suggestion but limited to product(s) they are dealing with. Therefore, it becomes necessary for you to know about each investment opportunity available with its **pros-n-cons**. That's my endeavor through this book.

To become wealthy, we shall be required to take many decisions relating to investments, return on investment, security of our hard-earned money, etc. However, the fact is, we are afraid of complex calculations that are required to reach the most logical decision especially when it comes to long-term investments. It's my personal experience that even highly qualified persons are afraid of taking decisions when it comes to financial issues.

Once you have sufficient knowledge about the subject, you will get the **confidence** to choose the investments which meet your requirements/objective thus giving you the **courage** to invest without fear.

"Happiness is not in the mere possession of money; it lies in the joy of achievement, in the thrill of creative effort."

-Franklin D. Roosevelt

2.
BASICS OF INVESTMENT

Let's start our journey of becoming "WEALTHY" by understanding the basics of Investments.

How to become wealthy?

In the journey to become wealthy, your focus should be to eliminate debts and create assets (investments are current assets) and not only on your monthly income. Try to take the following steps:

1. Save 15-20% of your monthly income every month:

The first step in the journey of wealth creation is to develop a habit of saving at least 15-20% of your monthly pay cheque no matter how much or how little you make. You may find it challenging initially when you start and therefore try to make a **'monthly budget'** for your household expenses. Review your budget, look at the expenses which can be eliminated or reduced, please do it to ensure that you are saving the targeted amount every month without fail.

2. Try to clear your debts:

In my personal opinion, you must keep the amount equivalent to your six months household expenditure in your savings account. For this purpose, try selecting the bank which gives higher interest rates or go for the auto-sweep option available with banks where they convert your savings account balance to Fixed Deposit and interest is payable on the FD rates for such deposits. However, this money always lies at your disposal and you can withdraw the amount as and when required. Amount over threshold limit in the Savings Account needs to be invested wisely. However, before going for the investments, try to clear your debts starting from high-interest loans e.g. Credit Card dues, Car loans, Personal loans, etc.

3. Start Investments as soon as possible and as much as you can:

Think of investing your surplus money on regular basis as soon as possible by selecting the investment option from the various alternatives available to you as discussed in this book. During interactions with my friends, I have observed that they always keep a good amount in their savings account yielding minimum returns (interest on savings account is lowest) only on the pretext that the money can be required to meet any unforeseen exigencies/emergencies and you may be one amongst them.

4. Avoid unnecessary expenses:

The key to becoming wealthy is to live a **'disciplined life'** i.e. you have made a monthly budget considering all the necessary expenses required to be incurred, please try to strictly follow the budget and don't get tempted to buy a higher-end mobile phone when your present smart phone is working properly or a new car when your old car is giving you no trouble. Designer cloths, costly watches, etc. shall be obstacles in your journey to becoming "wealthy" therefore become miser when it comes to spending money on such luxuries.

5. Make your long term Financial Goals:

Growing wealth is a long-term commitment. Make your long-term goals e.g. when the funds shall be required for children's higher education, daughter's marriage, the amount required for retirement corpus, etc., and start working on it with a firm commitment to stick to your "financial Planning". There will be moments when things will become tough, remind yourself that you have made your long-term goals and it's your wish to become wealthy.

> *"Money is multiplied in practical value depending on the number of W's you control in your life: what you do, when you do it, where you do it, and with whom you do it."*
>
> *-Tim Ferriss*

3.
WEALTH CREATION

Wealth Creation is a Mindset:

Always keep in mind that the journey to becoming wealthy doesn't start with huge money in your pocket. Wealth starts with the "right mindset". It's your choice to become wealthy therefore start saving a portion of your income regularly, avoid all unnecessary and avoidable expenditures, clear your debts as early as possible and keep in mind your long-term goals. Therefore, don't just focus on your income but your focus must be on investments and asset creation to fulfill all your dreams.

Steps to Wealth Creation:

Most of us want to become wealthy and debt-free but do not know how? Those who know how don't act on what they know. As the name implies, Wealth Creation means wealth has to be created and any creation requires creator, raw material, procedure, processes, etc. It's your choice to become wealthy i.e. you being the creator of the wealth, must invest your time, energies, and money to grow. There may be many strategies and steps to wealth creation; I will share the steps which I have followed to create wealth.

1. Develop a strong mindset:

Tony Robbins says *"80% of success is psychology"*. I strongly feel and have personally experienced that success first comes to your mind. It is your wish to become wealthy and you know for sure that this journey is long and challenging. A strong positive mindset will push you forward in your endeavors and will keep you focused and determined rather than giving up and you shall be willing to push through your challenges and get used to being uncomfortable because on the other side of being uncomfortable lies an "extraordinary life" which will be tension free.

2. Become Financially Educated:

During my interactions with highly educated people having vast experience in their respective areas of work, during their Retirement Planning sessions, I have observed that although they have come on the verge of retirement they are not clear about the basics of investments and so also not aware of investment schemes/opportunities available although, in my opinion, in your journey to "wealth creation", you have to start as early as possible

It is a fact that we don't learn about financial education in our school/colleges thus may not be aware of the ways and means of investment except few things told to us by friends and colleagues. Therefore, it is utmost necessary to learn about how money works by reading books, attending financial classes, the internet, etc. Invest your time and energies into learning about how to invest?

3. Develop S.M.A.R.T. Goals for Wealth Creation:

You must have a plan to achieve your goals e.g. buying a house/flat, children's education, daughter's marriage, retirement, etc. The plan must begin with deciding how much wealth you want to have, how you plan to get it when you will have it, and what you plan to give in return. Being from the teaching profession, I suggest setting S.M.A.R.T. Goals for wealth creation.

SPECIFIC – Try to make specific goals by asking the following questions to yourself:

- ❖ What are my goals?
- ❖ Why do I want to achieve them?
- ❖ Who are the people involved in my goal?

MEASURABLE – A measurable goal has a clear definition of success i.e. Target. You either hit the target or you don't, there is no in-between.

ACCOUNTABLE – Discuss your goals with your partners e.g. spouse and children and get their agreement. Agreeing upon goals with other people holds you accountable and accountability is vital to keeping with your goal of wealth creation. I discussed my dreams (goals) with my wife and children and happily lived simple life to help our dreams be fulfilled.

REALISTIC – Yes, it is always better to dream big but the risk is that if your goal is unrealistic, it becomes easier to give up on it. However, if you set a realistic and achievable goal, you are more likely to find ways to make it happen.

TIME FRAME – A goal without a specific time frame will not add a sense of urgency. Therefore, set a specific time frame to achieve the specific goal. This deadline will motivate you to be more intelligent with your time.

4. Be willing to take risks:

While doing my Masters in Economics, I often read that **"Profit is the reward of risk; higher the risk, higher the reward"** and applied this principle in investments many times by listening to my heart. Trusting and following your intuition is where the excitement is created. However, even for taking risks in investment, you require basic knowledge about the product, pros, and cons of a decision, gain vs. loss i.e. how much you can earn by taking the risk if you win and how much you will lose, if your decision goes wrong. Risk appetite changes with the age i.e. at a younger age you can take bigger risks whereas the same risks can't be taken when you are doing your retirement planning.

5. Increase Income:

The most obvious step to wealth creation is increasing your income. There are two forms of income: "Active and Passive". Active Income is income you receive from performing a service whereas Passive Income can be from a rental property, dividend, interest income, etc. **Warren Buffet has said, "If you don't find a way to make money while you sleep, you will work until you die."**

I presume you are intelligent and mature enough and know how to increase your active income, we will discuss in this book various ways and means to increase your passive income.

6. Start socializing and develop network:

Your environment dictates your performance, come out and surround yourself with people that perform at a much higher level than you, people that make you think outside the box and that make you think bigger and dream higher. Without making connections you are left on your own and the hardest way to attack business and life is alone. Connect yourself with as many people as possible. Go find out how you can connect with champions. The more time you spend with champions the easier it is for you to become a champion in health, wealth, and in life.

7. Create Your Legacy:

Giving money away to the less fortunate attracts more money back to you. You are signaling to God, the divine that you have more than enough and you can be trusted to be given more to do good things for others. In turn, you will be blessed with more money for your giving. In addition to money, give away time, free items, free consulting, etc., and watch the money flow back to you. Focus on how you can help others, not what you can get. When you feel you have enough to give, and you give to others, you feel more abundant, and you will attract more money.

Now you have the keys to wealth creation! It's time to unlock your path towards Healthy, Wealthy, and Prosperous life. Always remember it is your life and no one is coming to rescue you. Be prepared to participate in your own life and take continuous action. If you find change difficult, just take the first step. Just get moving and do something! If you do something you get somewhere but when you do nothing you get nowhere.

> *"Wealth is the ability to fully experience life."*
> *-Henry David Thoreau*

4.
INSURANCE

Before deliberating on investments, let us spend some time on Insurance related requirements which take a toll on your financial planning needs as you are always worried about your family's security in case any untoward incident happens with you or you or if any member of your family require medical treatment, which nowadays is very costly. What will happen in case of critical illness in the family and from where money will come? How much money I must keep in hand to take care of such exigencies?

The same is the case with a property also. In the recent past, Northern India witnessed many earth quakes, fortunately of low intensity but triggering fear in everybody's mind regarding the safety and security of their house/ flat, etc. What will happen if your property is damaged whereas you have spent all your hard-earned money in buying this property and wish to enjoy your peaceful life there after superannuation. In our journey of "wealth and wellbeing", we have to ensure our peace of mind also.

Insurance needs are also part of your investments as such insurance covers helps in sound Financial Planning.

4.1 LIFE INSURANCE

The most certain thing in life is "death". We know for sure that we have to die one day but the only dilemma is when! Though the average life in India is around 77 years, it is only a statistical number. Therefore, we are always worried if we are not there to support our family or loved ones who else will take care of them. Thus, we always look for the financial security of our loved ones especially when we are the breadwinners of our family.

Here comes the role of insurance agents. They meet you and assure you that you will live for many more years but you are afraid and need confidence. They tell you, we bet you live for another 20 years, you pay us only Rs.7000/- per annum and if anything goes wrong with you in next 20 years, we will pay your family Rs.50,00,000/- (example only). The proposal is lucrative! Isn't it! Suddenly a thought comes to your mind if nothing happens to me in the next 20 years whatever I will pay as a premium will be wasted. You then start searching for options where you get the life cover as well as your money back if you are alive.

Here comes the role of Insurance Agent, he will suggest you many such options and will convince you to take a policy where the premium is comparatively much higher than the pure term insurance policy but you will get a good amount on maturity. Most of us consider the second option i.e. insurance cover for life along with handsome maturity benefits and agree to pay a much higher premium than the simple term insurance policy. For better understanding have a look at how these insurance companies operate. The entire amount you pay as a premium is not what is invested. The premium you pay has three components:

- Expenses (including commissions paid to the agents as well as other administrative expenses and distribution costs)
- Mortality premium
- Investment Amount

Moreover, the amount permitted to be invested in equity may be around 10% of the total investment. Therefore you can't expect a great return from the insurance product when compared to several other investment options.

Your agents will never advise you to go for pure term insurance as each insurance product comes with an agent's commission ranging between 15 to 35 percent in the first year and therefore they will suggest you for a higher premium policy citing many benefits. It is often said that **"Insurance is never bought, but always sold"**.

Life insurance needs to depend on an individual's situation. Life insurance is an important piece of your financial planning if you have family who relies on you for financial support. In this book, we shall endeavor to invest your money wisely to make you wealthy, it is therefore suggested that term insurance is the cheapest and the best form of life insurance.

"I don't call it "Life Insurance", I call it "Love Insurance". We buy it because we want to leave a legacy for those we love."

-Author- unknown

4.2 MEDICAL INSURANCE

Most financial advisors suggest that having a health insurance plan is the starting point of all financial plans. Even before we start investing towards achieving goals, getting an adequate health insurance cover for self and family is of utmost necessity. Medical inflation in our country is around 17% as against general inflation of 6% currently.

When choosing the best health insurance policy, a lot of factors have to be weighed upon. Picking the right policy is as important as deciding to seek health policy coverage. Therefore, consider the following factors, before opting for the insured amount and type of coverage that you require:

Age:

Age plays an important role in determining the extent of the coverage you require. Younger people can opt for lower coverage policies and gradually increase them over the years. Since the probability of health problems increases with age and the chances of a claim being made also rises, the premium is costlier for older policyholders.

Health:

Your present health status is a critical determinant while deciding the health insurance coverage you would need. It is better to opt for a higher coverage amount, if you know that your ailment will worsen with age, choose a moderate coverage amount initially and increase it gradually to avoid being burdened by high premium payments all of a sudden.

Location:

The city in which you live weighs in on the costs of medical care facilities. Medical facilities in metropolitan cities are relatively more expensive than in tier 2/3 cities. Factor in such issues also while deciding the coverage amount.

Wealth & Wellbeing

The common medical insurance plans available today are as under:

Individual Plan:

An individual health plan is one whose benefits are available only to the one insured. This plan is suitable for people who are young and single and who are not having persistent health issues. The premium costs are generally lower and such policies provide coverage for hospitalization thus keeping them prepared for any medical exigency.

Family Floater Policy:

This is the most popular medical insurance policy in our country today as it provides security to the health risks of the entire family. Such policies are comprehensive schemes that provide coverage for people belonging to different age groups i.e. kids, adults, and older parents. Through one plan, policy holder can take care of the entire family instead of managing 3-4 policies and paying premiums separately.

Top-up & Super Top-up Policy:

Top-up Health Insurance policies are like a Stepney supporting you after the sum insured limit of your health insurance is exhausted. It is a kind of additional cover offered by the insurance companies to help you when you are out of your threshold limit. The basic health insurance policy and a top-up plan can be of two different companies. However, many insurance companies offer such policies in two different categories i.e. Top-up and Super-top policy. You can get a top-up health insurance policy at lower premiums, with the premium depending on the deductibles i.e. threshold limit. Although Top-up policies are comparatively cheaper than super top-up policies, it is always advisable to buy a super top-up policy for the reason as explained through the following example.

Rama has a Top-up and Super top-up policy with Rs.10 lacs cover and a regular medical insurance policy with a cover of Rs.5 lacs. He undergoes hospitalization treatment, consider the following scenarios:

MEDICAL BILL	TOP-UP POLICY	SUPER TOP-UP POLICY
The single bill comes to Rs. 7 lacs	Rs. 5 lacs by regular policy & Rs. 2 lacs by Top-up policy	Rs. 5 lacs by regular policy & Rs. 2 lacs by Super Top-up policy.
Two bills amounting to Rs.4.50 lacs each during the policy period	Rs. 5 lakh by regular policy and no amount from the top-up policy as the deductible is Rs.5 lacs.	Rs. 5 lacs by regular policy and Rs. 4 lacs by Super Top-up policy
Two bills of Rs. 7 lacs and Rs. 2 lacs during the policy period	Rs. 5 lacs by regular policy and Rs. 2 lacs by the top-up policy.	Rs. 5 lacs by regular policy and Rs. 2 lacs by the super top-up policy. Plus Rs. 2 lacs by the super top-up policy.

Health Insurance plans for Senior Citizens:

These plans are specifically designed for senior citizens to take care of the health care requirements that come with old age. Individuals between the age of 60 and 75 years can opt for these plans. The main benefits of senior citizen health insurance plans are cashless hospitalization cover, day care expenses and also pre-existing disease cover, etc.

Critical Illness Plans:

Critical illness insurance plans pay a lump sum on the diagnosis of any serious and long-term illness that requires the patient to undergo expensive treatment procedures. However, most health insurance plans provide a critical illness rider cover on paying an extra premium. You may think of strengthening your coverage by opting for standalone critical insurance, as it provides more comprehensive coverage.

Premium vis-à-vis Income:

It would not be advisable to go for a health cover policy whose premium is high enough to cause a dent in your budget. The basic purpose of a health insurance policy is to safeguard your health and finances during emergencies.

4.3 PERSONAL ACCIDENT COVER

While most of us are aware of Life Insurance and Health Insurance, very few are aware of Personal Accident Cover. Personal Accident schemes cover the policy holder against death or disability due to an accident. All general insurance companies offer these policies. As these are very low-priced policies, your agent will never discuss these policies. If you have sufficient life insurance with rider for personal accident cover and also have a health insurance policy, you may not think of it.

You must buy personal accident cover as this policy will provide financial support to the policy holder if he is disabled after an accident irrespective of the magnitude of an accident if you have ensured full coverage by paying a little extra premium over the basic personal accident insurance policy which covers death and permanent total disability. At around Rs. 750/- p.a. you can get personal accident insurance cover for Rs. 5 lacs which will cover death, permanent total disability, permanent partial disability, or temporary partial disability due to an accident i.e. Rs. 2/- per day only.

Salient Features of Personal Accident Insurance:

i) Personal Accident insurance includes much of what might not be covered by Health Insurance, such as rehabilitation, and is a great way to supplement existing coverage.
ii) Personal Accident Insurance usually does not require any medical underwriting.
iii) Personal Accident insurance can be inexpensive due to factors like where you live and how much coverage you want. It is a better option when traditional coverage is too expensive.
iv) For self-employed persons, it is a blessing in disguise as you may not have sick leave. Personal Accident Insurance could protect your finances during that time.
v) Personal Accident Insurance is ideal for those who intend to stay physically active and need the extra coverage even in the second innings of their lives when they are more prone to injuries.

4.4 PROPERTY INSURANCE

In the recent past, Northern India witnessed many earth quakes fortunately of lower intensity but triggering fears in the mind of people about the loss of their lives and property. As I am staying in a different city, I got a call from the Secretary of my housing society informing me that they are planning to insure the whole building of our society against earth quake and other such calamities and I have to pay my share of the premium. Although I have already insured my flat covering such calamities, I readily agreed to the proposal as I have to shell out a small amount for buying peace of mind as the comprehensive property insurance will also cover other amenities in the building.

I was surprised to know that most of the residents in our society had no property insurance whereas, in my opinion, it is extremely important to make sure that your property is safe and secure against a lot of mishaps. It is a safety measure that one must take to ensure that they have something to rely upon in times of distress that may occur due to property damage.

Property insurance is insurance that provides coverage for a building structure and its contents against natural or man-made calamities. However, coverage provided is not fixed and often varies depending on the type of insurance taken and the need of the client. The kinds of damages and losses covered will be mentioned in the policy document.

Although various types of property insurance are available the basic type of insurance is the one taken by homeowners that are taken for private residences and which ensures to back them up against a specific set of damages like fire, floods, earthquakes, theft, etc. Such basic cover is not very costly e.g. Rs. 1 crore property insurance for the above calamities will cost about Rs. 50,000/- approximately for insuring your property for 10 years. However, while buying property insurance, pick a policy that ensures maximum coverage and insures against more mishaps and misadventures while the premium is also affordable.

> *"Safety First is "Safety Always"*
> *-Charles Melville Hays*

5.
INFLATION

Inflation is an economic term that refers to an environment of generally rising prices of goods and services within a particular economy. With the rise of prices, the purchasing power of consumers' decreases i.e. same money in your hand will buy you less than what it was buying earlier. The measure of inflation over time is called the 'rate of inflation'.

For understanding and appreciating 'inflation', you need not listen to your grandparent's stories but you can feel it yourself when you compare the price of a particular item you were buying regularly for the last 5 years. The quality and quantity remaining the same, you are paying the higher price. You always complain that manufacturers are cheating you by increasing the price of their popular product but it is not the fact, even by keeping their margin the same, they are compelled to increase the price of the item as the raw material, wages, overhead, etc. are increased due to inflation.

Invest to stay ahead of Inflation:

We have listened to many stories that our ancestors were keeping their money by burying it in pots or by stuffing it under their bed but today if you save your money in the same way, you will lose money to inflation because the cost of living grows while the value of money does not. Earlier, the money was in the form of Gold, Silver, Bronze, etc. and these metals were inflation resistant because their value was also increasing with the rise in the cost of living.

It is, therefore, necessary to invest money wisely to ensure that your savings can beat inflation i.e. you are getting the money at maturity which is equal to or more than the inflation during the period so that your purchasing power remains intact.

Therefore, in a low-interest-rate environment, as we are experiencing today in our country, you could earn money in a Fixed Deposit but still lose purchasing power because of inflation and taxes, it can be termed as you are **"losing money safely"**.

As discussed above, 'inflation' is a rise in price levels. Economists believe that inflation comes about when the supply of money is greater than the demand for money. Inflation is viewed as a positive when it helps boost consumer demand and consumption thus driving economic growth. Anyone with loan benefits from inflation as it has the effect of eroding debt. You would have observed that now banks are offering long-term loans for buying a home/flat i.e. repayment tenure up to 30 years. It is a win-win situation for both i.e. lender and debtor as increased tenure will guarantee assured interest income for the lender for loan duration whereas due to 'inflation' the wages/earnings of the borrower will increase every year thus making the re-payment easier and less costly as the purchasing power of money will keep decreasing.

The average inflation in India (CPI) during the last five years was around 5.17% and last year it was 5.80%. Thus, for our investment purpose, we will presume 'average inflation' in our country will remain at 6%.

In layman's language, inflation is an increase in the value of goods and services over a certain period. Thus, for meeting our long term goals i.e. children marriage, purchase of flat or retirement planning, etc. we have to ensure that our investments must secure **'value of our money'** i.e. if we can buy any item for Rs.100/- today, the same will cost about Rs.180/- after 10 years (presuming inflation @ 6%p.a.). Therefore, our investment of Rs.100/- should give us the return equal to or more than Rs.80/- after 10 years to maintain the same purchasing power of our investment e.g. if we put our Rs.100/- in cumulative FD for 10 years at 7% interest, we will get Rs.200/- on maturity.

Time Value of Money:

The money you have in hand at the moment is worth more than the same amount you may get in the future mainly because of two reasons i.e. 'inflation' and its possible earning capacity. The relationship between the value of a rupee today and the value of a rupee in the future is known as 'Time Value of Money'. The value of the rupee received today is more as compared to the rupee received a year from now. Suppose your friend has borrowed Rs.10,000/- from you and promised to return it this month but he requests to allow him one more year time and in return, he will pay you Rs.10,500/-. If you are not in urgent need of money, you will most probably accept his proposal. Now, let's see the time value of money. If you would have invested Rs.10,000/- in fixed deposit for a year, you would have got Rs.10,700/- @ 7% interest p.a., thus you are getting Rs.200/- less than the present earning capacity of your money. It is therefore called Present Value (PV).

Moreover, let's take general inflation @ 6% per annum for example. i.e. what you could buy in Rs.10,000/- today, you will be required to pay Rs.10,600/- for the same stuff after a year, thus by getting back Rs.10,500/- after a year, you will be practically getting Rs. 9,900/- only in terms of money value. It is therefore called the 'Future Value" of money.

It is a fact that today's technology provides multiple calculations and applications to help you derive both the present value and future value of money. However, if you do not take the time to comprehend how these calculations are derived, you may make critical financial decisions using inaccurate data. As we are here for wealth creation, you must understand the following five variables:

1. Present Value (PV)

This is your current starting amount which is in your hands as of date i.e. your initial investment for your future.

2. Future Value (FV)

This will be your ending amount at a point in time in the future. It must be worth more than the present value, providing it is earning interest and growing over time.

3. The Number of Periods (N)

This is the timeline for your investment (or debts/loans). It is generally measured in years. Now a day, many banks are offering you a house loan for up to 30 years of repayment tenure. However, deciding the period for which you should take a loan is required to be derived carefully.

Let's understand this with an example:

Suppose you take a loan of Rs. 50,00.000/- at an interest rate of 9% p.a., how the Number of periods matters:

For 30 years tenure, your EMI will be Rs.40,231/- and you will be paying a total interest of Rs.94.83 lacs.

For 25 years tenure, your EMI will be Rs.41,960/- and you will be paying a total interest of Rs. 75.88 lacs.

For 20 years tenure, your EMI will be Rs. 44,986/- and you will be paying Rs. 57.97 lacs towards interest.

Thus, by paying only Rs. 1,729/- per month extra for 25 years tenure instead of 30 years, you will be saving Rs.18.95 lacs towards interest. Similarly, if you can afford an EMI of Rs. 44,986/- per month, you will be paying interest of Rs. 57.97 lacs only i.e. savings of Rs.36.86 lacs as compared to 30 years tenure loan.

4. Interest Rate (I)

This is the growth rate of your money over the lifetime of the investment. It is generally stated in percentage terms on yearly basis e.g. 7% per annum.

5. Equated Monthly Instalments (EMI)

This is the timeline for your investment or debts. It is usually measured in years but it can be quarterly, monthly, or daily.

There is a simple EXCEL function to calculate the EMI:

=EMI (rate, period, PV)

Rate: Interest rate per month

Period: Total tenure in months

PV: Present Value i.e. amount of loan/debt/investment

Suppose, you are taking a housing loan of Rs.25 lacs for 20 years at an interest rate of Rs. 8% p.a. The calculation will be as under:

=EMI (.08/12,20*12,2500000) i.e. Rs.20,911/- per month.

On many occasions, you have to make financial decisions that prevent you from investing and taking advantage of the time value of money concept. This is known as the opportunity cost of choosing a certain decision over another possible choice. Whenever you purchase any item on credit, you are deciding that whatever you purchased on credit was more valuable than a larger amount of future rupees, which is due to the interest you would have to pay on the loan amount. Therefore, it is necessary that before making any purchase decision on loan/credit, you need to ask yourself:

1. Is the purchase worth the extra payments towards the interest that I will have to make to pay it off?
2. Is the opportunity cost of giving up the potential earning of interest acceptable for my financial goals?
3. Is acquiring the desired item on credit is more meaningful to my financial freedom and security than saving and investing?

"Inflation destroys savings, impedes planning, and discourages investment. That means less productivity and a lower standard of living."

-Kevin Brady

6.
POWER OF COMPOUNDING

Compounding simply means that the interests you earn on your investment get re-invested and thereby you get interested in interest earned which leads to substantial growth in investments over the period. Although most of us know about compounding but don't know how it works? Compounding also depends on tenure on which interest is paid/credited to your account.

It is therefore important to know how the compounding is done on your investment i.e. whether it is quarterly (generally done by banks for cumulative FDs) or it is on a bi-yearly basis (as done for Government of India Bonds) or done yearly as is being done for NSC, KVP, etc. For example, if we have to invest Rs. 10 lacs for 5 years with safety, we will either go for bank cumulative FD for 5 years or NSC, and if the rate of interest is 7% p.a. in both the schemes. You will get Rs. 14,14,778/- on the maturity of your FD whereas you will get Rs.14,02,552/- only from the Post Office on the maturity of your NSC. Everything remains the same, the difference in maturity amount is due to the period of compounding.

The parameters that determine the power of compounding can be summarized as under:

a) Compounding rate
b) Time Duration
c) Tax rate
d) Growth Option

Let's quickly look at the KEY RULES to enjoy the power of compounding.

i) Starting Early:

As explained above, compounding is interest earned on the interest accrued on your investment over some time. Going by the example discussed above, we have seen that our investment has earned interest of Rs. 4,14,778/- when invested in the bank for five years. Assuming everything same, if we will invest the same amount for 10 years, our interest income will be Rs.10,01,597/- and not Rs. 8,29,556/- thus we will be earning Rs. 1,72,041/- more on our investment. Therefore, try to invest as early as possible even if they are for smaller amounts.

The best example of the power of compounding is Public Provident Fund Account only because of the tenure of investment (It is for 15 years and can be extended as many times as you desire in the intervals of 5 years extension each time). We shall discuss PPF separately. However, to appreciate the power of compounding, you must know that even a small investment of Rs. 10,000/- per month if started from the age of 25 years, will fetch you around Rs.1.75 Crores when you retire after the age of 60 years (calculated at the present rate of 7.1% p.a.).

ii) Discipline:

You have a goal to achieve be it your own home, children's education/marriage, your tension-free retired life, all that can be achieved only when you are disciplined about your investments. Warran Buffet once said, "Do not save what is left after spending, but spend what is left after saving".

iii) Be Patient:

Most of us wish for quick returns and many of us have lost our hard-earned income by investing in such schemes which gave false assurances of doubling the money in four-five years. Always remember that the powerful reap comes from the concept of compounding.

The best way of understanding the real value of your investment over some time is "Annualized Yield".

The average yield on an investment or a portfolio is the sum of all interest, dividends, or other income that the investment generates; divided by the age of the investment or the length of time the investor has held it. In particular, it's the yield or total income generated from any investment, divided by the number of years held.

The yield on fixed deposits includes compounded interest and other factors such as tax benefit till the end of the term. Here the calculation works in reverse. To get the yield on the interest that you will earn from FD, the total return earned on investment has to be divided by the number of invested years and then get the 'annualized effective yield'.

The bottom line is to start investing early, invest for a longer duration, be disciplined in your investments and be patient to achieve your long-term goals i.e. allow "power of compounding" to generate wealth for you when you are sleeping.

> *"The Compound Effect is the principle of reaping huge rewards from a series of small, smart choices."*
>
> *-Darren Hardy*

7.
INVESTMENT PLANNING

Investment planning is the process of aligning your financial goals and objectives with your financial resources. We have already discussed S.M.A.R.T. goals. Now is the time to plan your investments to each specific goal in the most efficient manner. It is also important to define a specific timeline and how much risk you are willing to take on to determine your optimal asset allocation.

Investment is a personal decision-making process and depends on numerous factors such as your age, your responsibilities, marital status, and monthly income and life stages. Therefore, the investment portfolio varies for each e.g. portfolio of a young individual will be different from a middle-aged person with the responsibility of the family on his head and it will be different for a person nearing retirement.

Let's discuss step by step the investment planning process:

Step One: Define your goals and objectives:

The first step in the investment planning process is to define your goals. As already discussed each goal must be specific, realistic, and have a time limit e.g. buying a flat/home, daughter's marriage, retirement planning, etc. You must also define your goal timeline or time horizon. There may be times when you want to see quick growth or are you may be interested in seeing investments growth over time.

Step Two: Assess your Current Financial position:

The next most important step in the investment planning process is to define your present financial situation. You must figure out how much money you have to invest. The best way of assessing your financial position is by making a budget to evaluate your monthly disposable income after expenses and keeping some money to meet emergencies/exigencies. It may look little tedious job at the beginning but shall give you a fair idea to determine how much money you can spare for investments without compromising on your lifestyle.

Further, it is also important to consider how accessible you need your investments to be. If you might need to cash in on your investment quickly, you would want to invest in more liquid assets e.g. stocks or FDs, rather than in fixed assets like Real Estate.

Step Three: Determine your Risk Tolerance:

The next important step in your investment planning is to decide your risk appetite. Generally, at a younger age, you can take more risks since your portfolio has time to recover from losses if any. However, if you are older, you should look for less risky investments.

It is a fact that riskier investments have the potential for significant returns but also major losses. Putting money on undervalued stock or piece of land could prove fruitful but you could lose your investment. It is, therefore, suggested that if you are looking to build wealth over some time, you may choose a safer investment path.

I read about the "Rule of 100" for investments, it is a very popular thumb rule for asset allocation based on the life cycle of individuals. In this rule, one has to subtract his age from 100 and that proportion becomes the proportion of investment in equity e.g. a young single, working individual at the age of 25 should invest 75% in equities but for a 45-year-old, married person, the investment in equities should not be more than 55%. However, it is only an asset allocation tool, and depending on the risk tolerance and life stages of an individual, investment planning may be done as under:-

Stage 1 – Career Commencement:

This is a stage when you begin your career and at a young age do not have major responsibilities. Therefore, your risk tolerance is high, and therefore can safely invest 75-80% in equities. However, the choice of investments should include both direct equity and mutual funds, IPOs, and even real estate.

Stage 2 – Getting Married:

This is a very important stage in a person's life as expenses start increasing after marriage and financial responsibilities change and so do the investment objectives. This is a period of capital appreciation, therefore, investment in high growth equities is recommended at this stage.

Stage 3 – Becoming Parents:

Parenthood is one of the most joyous times in one's life, but also increases responsibilities. The risk appetite becomes lower at this stage, therefore, investment to the tune of 35-40% may be considered in debt funds.

Stage 4 – Consolidation:

This is the stage between the age of 40-55 years when the children start growing older and needs for higher education increase. At this stage, it is highly recommended to tone down your equity exposure and increase investments in debt and liquid instruments. At this stage, your focus should be on capital preservation and investment in balanced funds may be a preferred choice.

Stage 5 – Retirement:

This is the last stage of investment planning when individuals have to invest for their post-retirement life. At this stage, investments must be in liquid funds where safety and returns are guaranteed as your "Active Income" may seize after retirement and you must have sufficient corpus to survive for another 20-25 years after retirement. We shall deal with this stage of investment planning with examples a little later.

Step Four - Decide where to invest in:

The final step in investment planning is to decide where to invest. There are many options available to you for putting your hard-earned money e.g. stocks, mutual funds, FDs, Post Office Schemes, real estate, etc. Your budget, goals, and risk tolerance will guide you toward the right type of investment for you. However, one thing that must always be kept in mind is that your portfolio should be diversified e.g. don't put all of your money into stocks for higher gains and take risk of losing everything if the stock market crashes. It is therefore advisable to allocate your assets to a few different investment types that fit in with your goals and risk tolerance to maximize your growth and stability.

Step Five – Monitor your Investments:

This is the most crucial stage in investment planning. Once you have made your investments, it's not advisable to leave them alone. At regular intervals, you should check in to see how your investments are performing and decide if you need to re-balance. For example, you are not putting enough money into your investments monthly and you are not on the track to reach your goals or maybe you're depositing more than you need to and you're ahead of schedule. Maybe you want to move your money to a more stable investment as you get closer to achieving your long-term goals.

It's equally important to go through the assessment steps that you followed to create your "Investment Plan" every few years to ensure everything is going according to plan. If required, make changes or adjustments necessary to continue working towards your goals and objectives.

Becoming a good investor requires research and experience. If it's a first-time investing, the experience will come, so focus on soaking in information about the different types of investments that are available to you. To help you in choosing the right investment, different investment options available are discussed in this book. A key to successful investing is not putting all of your eggs in one basket and therefore the mantra is "diversify, diversify & diversify".

"In investing, what is comfortable is rarely profitable."
-Robert Arnott

8.
CONTINGENCY FUNDS

Life being unpredictable can throw surprises and catch you off-guard at any time e.g. emergency medical expenses, natural disaster or losing your only job, etc. Not anticipating beforehand for such situations not only puts you in a difficult situation at those moments but also derails your plans as you are forced to either dip into your savings or take on additional debt. Therefore, planning for such a situation is extremely necessary and makes it an important part of any "Financial Planning".

A contingency fund is commonly known as an "emergency fund" is hence a fund that is designed to be used for meeting any unforeseen emergencies and may be either in cash or liquid assets. The primary objective of a contingency fund is to enhance your financial stability and to protect your financial plan in such cases of emergencies. This also helps you in avoiding high-interest options such as credit cards.

The size of the contingency fund depends upon the regularities and stabilities of income, risk management in terms of whether you have adequate insurance cover for life and health, health condition, number of dependents, and assets under possession. As discussed earlier, the thumb rule is to have the contingency fund that you can live comfortably for around 6 months without any income, in case of any emergency. Many households have witnessed stressful situations during this pandemic which kept them away from their business/job for such a long duration.

Advantages of a Contingency Fund:

1. Contingency Funds protects you from taking an additional loan:

As emergencies can't be predicted, you may not have sufficient cash readily available to meet the exigency if you have not maintained a contingency fund. You will therefore be forced to avail loan or avail of the credit card limit available to you. However, it will attract interest at much higher rates. This additional burden of repayment of loan and interest may jeopardize your investment planning for years.

2. Contingency funds help you to finance major emergencies:

A contingency fund will help you in meeting emergency fund requirements without disturbing your day-to-day expenses, your long-term financial plans, your children's education, retirement planning, or even your dream vacation. It offers you the capability to meet large cash requirements with very little disturbance to your day-to-day life. The absence of such funds may create havoc in your life e.g. medical condition of any member of family/parents, natural disasters, damage to your property, etc. which may have severe outcomes.

3. Contingency funds help you to meet large expenses in unforeseen circumstances:

The importance of a contingency fund is not only limited to meeting unexpected liquidity requirements. The fund may also be used to meet large expenses in case you wish to switch jobs and there is a gap or dent in your primary source of income like it happened during the pandemic. However, it is advisable to use contingency funds in crises only and may not be spent for other uses.

Please be aware that contingency funds always generate lesser returns because of their liquid nature so do not keep aside more funds than what you may need for contingency funds. However, on the other hand, having very few contingency funds than what is required would land you in trouble. Therefore, contingency funds should also be properly planned keeping in view your responsibilities/liabilities, present income, risk tolerance, size of family/dependents, etc.

FLEXY DEPOSITS:

Although the need of withdrawing money from time to time for your regular monthly expenses and so also to meet contingencies, if any, you keep sufficient balance in your savings account which attracts interest at 2.5% to 4% whereas the current inflation is around 6% per annum. Thus, the actual return on your savings account balance becomes negative which means your money is being eaten away by inflation.

The solution to this problem is 'Flexi Deposit'. A Flexi deposit is a special kind of deposit scheme offered by banks. In Flexi-deposit, the depositor opting for a Flexi deposit gets the benefit of both the liquidity of savings accounts and the high returns of fixed deposits. Many banks in India offer Flexi-deposit schemes to customers e.g. SBI, BOB, ICICI, BOI, Axis Bank, etc.

Benefits of Flexi-Deposit savings account:

Flexi deposits offer a host of features and benefits to account holders such as:

a. Attractive Interest:

Flexi deposits earn higher interest compared to Savings Accounts, enabling you to earn more through your money.

b. Flexible Tenures:

Different banks have different tenures for the flexi deposit schemes, ensuring one finds a tenure that best suits his financial needs.

c. Investment Amount:

Individuals can choose the amount they intend to deposit. In many banks, the balance in your savings accounts above the threshold decided by you is automatically transferred to the FD account.

d. Premature Withdrawal:

Unlike Fixed Deposits, in such Flexi-deposits, you can withdraw any amount from your savings account including in such Flexi FDs as and when required through cheque, cash, ATM, etc.

e. Easy to Open:

The Flexi-deposit accounts are opened like Savings Accounts. If you already have a savings account, you can request your bank in writing to convert your existing savings account to a Flexi deposit account.

f. Auto-renewal of Fixed Deposits:

Banks generally allow auto-renewal of Flexi FDs, ensuring account holders don't have to worry about renewal.

"Optimism research teaches us that we should expect the best and have a contingency plan for the worst."

-Paul Dolan

9.
ASSET ALLOCATION

Asset allocation refers to diversifying your investments among a variety of different types of assets. It helps protect you from large losses in your portfolio. An "asset" can be anything from your cash, jewelry, fixed deposits, home, car, etc. However, generally "asset allocation" refers to putting your money in diversified investments.

Asset allocation means that you spread your money among different assets, such as equities, mutual funds, fixed-income, and cash equivalents. Each of these responds differently to different trends in the market. Therefore, having a blend of them in your portfolio will help you minimize losses in a market downturn or dip in interest rates as happened recently when the interest rates are continuously going down.

The Asset allocation decision mainly depends on three factors:

a. Your Investment Objective
b. Time Horizon
c. Your Risk Tolerance

Depending on your age, lifestyle, family commitments, your financial goal/investments objectives will vary. Therefore, first, you need to define your investment objectives with specific timelines e.g. buying a house/flat, buying a new car, paying for your children's higher education, daughter's marriage, retirement planning, etc.

What Is Asset Allocation?

Asset allocation means that you spread your money among different assets, such as Fixed Deposits, Recurring Deposits, PF, PPF, NPS, equities, mutual funds, jewelry, real estate, and other cash equivalents. Each of these responds differently to different trends in the market. Therefore, having a blend of them in your portfolio will help you minimize losses in case of a market downturn.

We have already discussed the power of compounding. Therefore, for higher returns in a long time duration with the least risk, you may consider Kisan Vikas Patra, a Post Office saving, where the annualized yield today is around 10% for one-time investment for a longer duration.

Similarly, for systematic investment for a longer duration, you may consider opening PPF Account e.g. if you wish to plan for retirement, start depositing Rs.12,500/- every month in PPF a/c and after 30 years, you will get approximately Rs.1.50 crores at present interest rates that too completely tax-free. Moreover, you will get a rebate under Section 80C of the IT Act for the deposit made by you in PPF a/c every year. Further, the interest earned in PPF a/c is also exempted.

However, at a younger age, you may go for equities and mutual funds as per the rule of 100 already discussed. Systematic Investment Plan (SIP) is in thing today and you may consider investing in equities through Mutual Funds via SIP instead of directly investing in equities that carry maximum risk.

We shall discuss in detail all investment options with their pros-n-cons to help you consider the best investments for you considering the factors mentioned above i.e. your goal(s), time horizon, and risk tolerance capacity.

"The enemy of a good asset allocation is the quest for a perfect one. Fight the urge to be Perfect."

-Richard A. Ferri

10.
OBTAIN PAN CARD

The importance of PAN CARD introduced in 1972 has grown over time, and today it is an essential requirement for any financial transaction. It will be very difficult to invest your money without PAN Card.

PAN (Permanent Account Number) is an identification number assigned to all taxpayers in India. PAN is an electronic system through which all tax-related information for a person/company is recorded against a single PAN number. This acts as the primary key for the storage of information shared across the country. Hence no two tax-paying entities can have the same PAN.

PAN is issued by the Income Tax Department, Government of India, and is valid for a lifetime once issued. PAN has around 25 crores enrolments as of date. PAN Card is issued to individuals, companies, non-resident Indians, or anyone who pays taxes in India.

Type of PAN:

1. Individual
2. HUF (Hindu Undivided Family)
3. Company
4. Firms / Partnerships
5. Trusts
6. Society
7. Foreigners

Enrolment for PAN:

You can enroll for PAN in 3 simple steps, online or offline. For obtaining PAN, you require only two types of documents i.e. POA

(Proof of Address) and POI (Proof of Identity). For an individual, POA/POI can be Adhaar Card, Passport, Voter ID, or Driving Licence. However, for foreigners, the documents required are PIO / OCI Card issued by the Indian Government, Bank Statement of the residential country, copy of the NRE bank Statement in India. The cost of a PAN Card is Rs.110/- or Rs. 1,020/- (approximately) if PAN card is to be dispatched outside India. The PAN card is generally dispatched in 15 days.

Online	Offline
Visit NSDL or UTIITSL website	Get an application form from the authorized PAN Centre
Fill Form, Submit the required documents and pay fees	Fill out the form, attach required documents & submit along with fees
PAN will be sent to the given address	PAN will be sent to the given address

How to Update / Edit PAN Details:

PAN can be updated by the following steps:

- Go to the NSDL website and select the update PAN section
- Select option "Correction" in the existing PAN date. (A copy of the supporting documents (POI/POA) is required)

Duplicate PAN Card:

If you have lost your PAN card, apply for a duplicate PAN card online or offline. Login to NSDL or UTIITSL website, fill the form 49-A for Indian citizens or Form 49-AA for foreigners and make the payment online for a duplicate copy of your PAN card. The duplicate PAN will be generally dispatched within 45 days.

Why do you need PAN Card?

PAN is a unique identification number that enables each tax-paying entity of India with the following:

1. Proof of Identity
2. Proof of Address
3. Mandatory for filing Income Tax Return

4. Registration of business
5. Financial transactions
6. Eligibility to open and operate bank accounts
7. Phone / Gas connection
8. PAN is beneficial to complete e-KYC for mutual fund investments

PAN for e-KYC (KNOW YOUR CUSTOMER)

PAN to Aadhaar linking is mandatory for e-KYC and verification to avail services and benefits from respective service providers. The e-KYC process is paperless enabling a service provider to manage documents easily and effectively. Besides being quick and secure, information shared by e-KYC contains authenticated data making it legal and acceptable for the parties involved in the transaction. Further, the entire system is paperless and online eliminating the physical movement of information making it a cost-effective and time-saving process.

11.
TAX DEDUCTIONS

Before we discuss or plan your portfolio of investments, please note that it is not what you earn that matters, but what you keep does. Taxes, If not planned well, will take away a major portion of your earnings. It is, therefore, necessary to plan properly for your taxes and look into the deductions which are mentioned in the Income Tax Act, 1961.

Let's look at section 80 of the Income Tax Act allowing certain deductions and exemptions to individuals or a Hindu Undivided Family (HUF):

Section	Deduction on	Allowed Limit (maximum) FY 2018-19
80C	Investment in PPF – Employee's share of PF – NSCs – Life Insurance Premium – Children's Tuition Fee – Principal Repayment of home loan – Investment in Sukanya Samridhi Account – ULIPS – ELSS – Sum paid to purchase a deferred annuity – Five-year deposit scheme – Senior Citizens savings scheme – Subscription to notified securities/notified deposits scheme – Contribution to notified Pension Fund – Few others	Rs. 1,50,000

80CCD(1B)	Additional contribution to NPS	Rs. 50,000
80TTA(1)	Interest Income from Savings account	Maximum up to 10,000
80TTB	Exemption of interest from banks, post offices, etc. Applicable only to senior citizens	Maximum up to 50,000
80GG	For rent paid when HRA is not received from the employer	Least of: – Rent paid minus 10% of total income – Rs. 5000/- per month – 25% of total income
80E	Interest on education loan	Interest paid for 8 years
80EE	Interest on home loan for first-time homeowners	Rs 50,000
80D	Medical Insurance – Self, spouse, children Medical Insurance – Parents more than 60 years old or (from FY 2015-16) uninsured parents more than 80 years old	– Rs. 25,000 – Rs. 50,000
80DD	Medical treatment for handicapped dependent or payment to specified scheme for maintenance of a handicapped dependent – Disability is 40% or more but less than 80% – Disability is 80% or more	– Rs. 75,000 – Rs. 1,25,000
80DDB	Medical Expenditure on Self or Dependent Relative for diseases specified in Rule 11DD – For less than 60 years old – For more than 60 years old Diseases covered: Neurological Diseases (where the disability level has been certified as 40% or more) Parkinson's Disease Malignant Cancers AIDS Chronic Renal Failure Hemophilia Thalassemia	Lower of Rs 40,000 or the amount paid – Lower of Rs 1,00,000 or the amount paid
80U	Self-suffering from disability: – An individual suffering from a physical disability (including blindness) or mental retardation. – An individual suffering from severe disability	– Rs. 75,000 – Rs. 1,25,000
80RRB	Deductions on Income by way of Royalty of a Patent	Lower of Rs 3,00,000 or income received

How to calculate deductions u/s 80C?

For section 80C, the amount of eligible investment or expenditure as specified is fully allowed for deduction subject to the limit of Rs. 1,50 lacs. Section 80CCD (1b) provides an additional deduction of Rs.50,000/- for a contribution towards NPS, Atal Pension Yojana, etc. Thus, the total of deductions including 80C and 80CCd (1b) can be a maximum of Rs. 2 lakh for a single year. However, salaried persons can avail of further deduction up to 10% of their salary (Basic+DA) for contributions made by their employers for NPS.

Further, please note that as per Budget 2020, any contribution towards EPF, NPS, and Superannuation Fund will be added to the salary as "perquisites" and taxable under salaries in the hands of employees.

Rebate u/s 87A of Income Tax Act:

A rebate u/s 87A is one of the income tax provisions that help low-income earning taxpayers reduce their income tax liability. Taxpayers earning an income below a certain limit have the benefit of paying marginally lower taxes. A Taxpayers can claim the benefit of rebate u/s 87A for FY 2019-20 AND 2020-21 only if the following conditions are satisfied:

He is a resident individual

His total income after reducing the deductions under chapter VI-A (Section 80C, 80D, and so on) does not exceed Rs. 5 lakh in Financial Year.

The tax rebate is limited to Rs.12,500/-. This means, if your total tax payable is less than Rs.12,500, then you will not have to pay any tax. Please note that the rebate will be applied to the total tax before adding the health and education cess of 4%.

Following are some investment options allowing deductions under section 80C. They may help you in growing your money besides saving taxes:-

Investment options	Average Interest	Lock-in period for	Risk factor
ELSS funds	12% – 15%	3 years	High
NPS Scheme	8% – 10%	Till 60 years of age	High
ULIP	8% – 10%	5 years	Medium
Tax saving FD	6% – 7%	5 years	Low
PPF	7.10%	5 years	Low
Senior citizen savings scheme	7.4%	5 years (can be extended for other 3 years)	Low
National Savings Cert.	6.8%	5 years	Low
Sukanya Samriddhi Yojna	7.6%	Till girl child reaches 21 years of age (partial withdrawal allowed when she reached 18 years)	Low

12.
FILING OF INCOME TAX RETURNS

As per Income Tax Act, 1961, Income tax is imposed by the Government of India on anybody who earns in India. Any individual, whose total income exceeds the exemption limit before allowing for deductions; have to file their Income Tax returns commonly known as "ITR".

Let's understand the jargon used to define periods as per Income Tax Act:

FINANCIAL YEAR (FY)
The financial year starts from 1st April and ends on 31st March. All the finance-related transactions within this duration of one year are considered for income tax purposes.

ASSESSMENT YEAR (AY)
The income of a particular financial year is assessed in the following financial year, which is known as the Assessment Year. E.g. For the financial year 2020-21, the assessment year shall be 2021-22.

PREVIOUS YEAR (PY)
As per income tax provisions, the previous year is the financial year for which your income is being assessed.

The five income heads under Income Tax Act:

1. Income from salary:
Income from salary includes wages, pension, annuity, gratuity, fees, commission, profits, leave encashment, annual accretion,

and transferred balance in recognized Provident Fund (PF) and contribution to employees' pension account.

2. Income from house property:

Rental incomes from properties owned by a person other than those which are occupied by him are charged as income from house property. If the property is vacant then a notional income is included under this head. Under this, income received from rental proceeds after 30% standard deduction is considered.

3. Income from business/profession:

Income from business or profession includes profit/loss from a business entity or a profession, any interest, salary, or bonus to a partner of a firm.

4. Capital Gains:

Income from capital gains includes long-term capital gains (LTCG) and short-term capital gains (STCG) on the sale of any capital assets. Under this profit from the sale of real estate, stocks, mutual funds, gold, etc. is covered.

5. Income from other sources:

Income from other sources includes interest on bank deposits and securities, dividends, royalty income, winning on lotteries and races, and gifts received among others.

The Tax Slabs for General Tax Payers (Indian Residents) for the financial year 2020-21 are as under: (For men & women below 60 years)

TAXABLE INCOME	TAX RATE (existing scheme)	TAX RATE (new scheme)
Up to Rs. 2,50,000	Nil	Nil
Rs. 2,50,001 to Rs. 5,00,000	5%	5%
Rs. 5,00,001 to Rs. 7,50,000	20%	10%
Rs. 7,50,001 to Rs. 10,00,000	20%	15%
Rs. 10,00,001 to Rs. 12,50,000	30%	20%
Rs. 12,50,001 to Rs. 15,00,000	30%	25%
Above Rs. 15,00,000	30%	30%

Filing Of Income Tax Returns

Income Tax Slabs for Senior Citizens (Aged 60 years & above but below 80 years)

TAXABLE INCOME	TAX RATE (existing scheme)	TAX RATE (new scheme)
Up to Rs. 2,50,000	Nil	Nil
Rs. 2,50,001 to Rs. 3,00,000	Nil	5%
Rs. 3,00,001 to Rs. 5,00,000	5%	5%
Rs. 5,00,001 to Rs. 7,50,000	20%	10%
Rs. 7,50,001 to Rs. 10,00,000	20%	15%
Rs. 10,00,001 to Rs. 12,50,000	30%	20%
Rs. 12,50,001 to Rs. 15,00,000	30%	25%
Above Rs. 15,00,000	30%	30%

Tax Slabs for Very Senior Citizens (Above 80 years)

TAXABLE INCOME	TAX RATE (existing scheme)	TAX RATE (new scheme)
Up to Rs. 2,50,000	Nil	Nil
Rs. 2,50,001 to Rs. 5,00,000	Nil	5%
Rs. 5,00,001 to Rs. 7,50,000	20%	10%
Rs. 7,50,001 to Rs. 10,00,000	20%	15%
Rs. 10,00,001 to Rs. 12,50,000	30%	20%
Rs. 12,50,001 to Rs. 15,00,000	30%	25%
Above Rs. 15,00,000	30%	30%

Surcharge:

a) 10% of Income Tax where total income exceeds Rs. 50 lacs
b) 15% of Income Tax where total income exceeds Rs. 1 crore
c) 25% of Income Tax where total income exceeds Rs. 2 crore
d) 37% of Income Tax where total income exceeds Rs. 5 crore

Education Cess: 4% of Income-tax plus surcharge.

Before proceeding further, let's take a look at the New Scheme which is optional for individuals and HUF.

Individuals and HUF taxpayers are eligible to choose a new tax regime from FY 2020-21 with lower tax rates and zero deductions/

exemptions. The Budget 2020 introduces a new regime under section 115BAC giving an option to individuals to pay income tax at lower rates. The new system is applicable for income earned from 1st April 2020 (FY 2020-21). The new tax regime does not allow 70 deductions and exemptions. Thus, the new tax regime saves taxes for taxpayers who don't claim any deductions or exemptions.

From a tax planning perspective, it is essential to choose the tax regime at the beginning of the financial year. A taxpayer must make a comparison of the income tax under the new tax regime with the existing regime. Once the taxpayer chooses the new tax regime at the beginning of the year, the investments and TDS or advance tax payable calculations are made accordingly. The taxpayer has to furnish FORM 10IE to the Income Tax Department before filing the return if the taxpayer intends to opt for the new tax regime.

In case an individual claims lower deductions for tax savings, towards health insurance, investment in PPF, NPS, and so on, the new regime will be more beneficial against individuals who utilize the tax-saving investments.

Generally, individuals with an income bracket between Rs.5-10 lakh with the lower claim of deductions will benefit from the new scheme whereas individuals with higher income can benefit more from the existing regime by making tax-saving investments.

However, each taxpayer must calculate income tax, taking into account their tax-saving investments, and then choose the regime.

A salaried taxpayer can choose the new tax regime at the beginning of FY 2020-21 and intimate their employer which will be irrevocable. However, the change that can be done at the time of filing the ITR is July 2021. (This year, the last date for filing ITR has been extended up to 30th September 2021). Salaried employees can opt-in and opt-out every year.

A non-salaried taxpayer has to choose the new regime at the time of filing the tax return. Once a non-salaried opts out of the new tax regime, he cannot opt-in again for the new tax regime in the future.

FILING OF IT RETURN:

Filing of tax returns in India is mandatory for individuals only when their taxable income exceeds Rs.2,50,000/- Please note, if your taxable income is Rs. 4,00,000/- and you have invested Rs. 1.50 lakh in investment schemes specified under Section 80C then you will have to pay no taxes but still you will be required to file a NIL return. If you have undertaken foreign travel for over Rs.2,00,000, you will be required to file a tax return.

Benefits of Filing Returns:

1. Claiming a Tax refund:

Certain passive income such as term deposit interest or dividend income suffers tax deduction at the source. It may be exempted for many individuals if it is below the threshold limit. Excess taxes paid by an individual either by way of tax deduction or advance/self-assessment tax can be refunded only by filing for tax returns. By filing an ITR online, the refund of taxes can be claimed in the individual's bank account that is KYC-compliant.

2. Processing of Documents:

ITR is a key document for processing applications for various purposes e.g. for processing of house or auto loan. Besides securing a loan, the income tax return helps in the processing of obtaining credit cards, insurance policies, etc. The fact that you are filing your ITR regularly gives you faster access to credit at better terms.

3. Application for VISA:

The tax return filing ensures in smooth processing of VISA applications as immigration authorities then deem the individual as tax-compliant. Certain embassies e.g. US, Canada, UK, etc. are particular about the tax return records of the individual.

4. Claiming Losses:

Filing of tax return within the due date is mandatory to claim specified losses for an individual taxpayer, such as losses from capital gains, business or profession, etc. It also serves as a document to track losses that can be claimed in the future e.g. an individual taxpayer who makes a profit from the sale of mutual funds or equity shares can adjust these profits with losses incurred in the past by filing tax returns on time.

5. Serves as proof of Income:

Self-employed taxpayers do not have any proof of income, unlike salaried individuals who receive a salary certificate in Form 16. Therefore, the ITR serves as proof of income for these self-employed taxpayers. ITR is considered as authorized income proof all over the world. If you are looking for higher education or employment abroad, ITR is largely accepted as income proof.

Applicable Returns & Forms:

An individual resident who is 60 years or above in age but less than 80 years at any time during the previous year is considered a Senior Citizen for Income Tax purposes. A super Citizen is an individual resident who is 80 years or above.

Section 194P of the IT Act, 1961 introduced from 1st April 2021 provides the following conditions for exempting Senior Citizens from filing income tax returns aged 75 years and above:

- Senior Citizen should be of age 75 years or above
- Senior Citizen should be 'Resident' in the previous year
- Senior Citizen has a pension and interest income only & interest income accrued/earned from the same specified bank in which he is receiving his pension.

ITR-1 (SAHAJ) – Applicable for Individual:

This return is applicable for a Resident Individual having total income from any of the following sources up to Rs. 50 lakh:

a. Salary / Pension
b. One House Property
c. Other Sources (interest, dividend, Family Pension, etc.)
d. Agricultural Income up to Rs. 5,000/-

ITR – 2 – Applicable for Individuals and HUF

This return is applicable for Individual and Hindu Undivided Family (HUF) not having income under the head Profits or Gains of Business or Profession and who is not eligible for filing ITR-1.

ITR – 3 – Applicable for Individuals and HUF

This return is applicable for Individual and HUF having income under the head of Profits or Gains of Business or Profession and who is not eligible for filing ITR-1, 2, or 4.

ITR-4 (SUGAM) – Applicable for Individual, HUF & Firm:

This return is applicable for a resident Individual, HUF, or a Firm (other than LLP) having a total Income up to Rs. 50 lakh and having Income from Business and Profession which is computed on a presumptive basis and income from any of the following sources:

a. Salary / Pension
b. One House Property
c. Other Sources (interest, dividend, Family Pension, etc.)
d. Agricultural Income up to Rs. 5,000/-
e. Income from Business/Profession computed on a presumptive basis

Form 15 G and Form 15H:

Form 15G and Form 15H are self-declaration forms that an individual submits to the bank requesting not to deduct TDS on interest income as their income is below the basic exemption limit. Providing PAN is compulsory for availing of this exemption.

Form 15G is for Resident Individual or HUF with age less than 60 years and tax calculated on your total income is NIL. Further, the total interest income for the year is less than the basic exemption limit of that year i.e. 2.5 lakh for FY 2020-21.

Form 15 H is applicable for Resident Individuals of 60 years and above and if your total taxable income is NIL.

Income Tax e-refund:

The income Tax Department has discontinued issuing refunds by cheques and issues refunds only as an e-refund. To receive the refund amount, your bank account should be linked to PAN and should have been pre-validated on the income tax e-filing portal.

You are required to visit the e-filing portal of the IT Department with your user name and password. Those who have not registered with the IT e-filing portal need to register themselves beforehand.

As an assessee, it is important for you to first link your PAN to your bank account to be able to pre-validate the bank account. You can e-verify the Income Tax Return only by using a pre-validated bank account.

Timely filing of IT Return:

Generally, the last date of filing IT returns for persons not required to be audited is 31st July and for persons required to be audited is 30th September every year. However, the Government at times gives some relaxation in these dates due to prevailing conditions e.g. for FY 20-21 last dates have been extended to 30th September and 30th November 2021 respectively for filing IT returns.

Although the due dates for filing the Income Tax Returns for AY 2021-22 have been extended, there is no relief provided from the interest chargeable under Section 234A if the self-assessment tax liability exceeds Rs. 1 lakh (net of Advance Tax and TDS, if any).

Apart from the penalty levied by the IT Department, there are other consequences that a taxpayer may face for late filing of returns:

i. Unable to set off losses:

Losses incurred (other than house property loss) are not allowed to be carried forward to subsequent years. You cannot set off these losses against future gains if the return has not been filed within the due date.

ii. Interest on the delay of filing return:

Apart from the penalty for late filing, interest under section 234A at 1% per month or part thereof till the date of payment of taxes.

iii. Delayed Refunds:

In case you're entitled to receiving a refund for excesses taxes paid, you must file the returns before the due date to receive your refund at the earliest.

13.
PUBLIC PROVIDENT FUND

The PPF account or Public Provident Fund Scheme is one of the most popular long-term saving-cum-investment products, mainly due to its combination of safety, returns, and tax savings. The PPF scheme was introduced in the year 1968 by the Government of India. As of date, the amount you invest up to Rs.1,50,000/- is deductible from your taxable income, the interest you earn is non-taxable and the maturity amount you get after 15 years is also tax-exempt.

I prefer PPF Account for one major reason i.e. **"peace of mind"**. Once you have maintained the account for 7 years, you will always be confident that in case of any exigency/emergency, you may get 50% of your savings up to 6 years 'within minutes' to meet the exigency. That will give you big relief when you are planning for other long-term investments. The main benefits of the PPF scheme:

1. Risk-free, guaranteed returns:

The PPF is backed by the Government of India thus it is entirely risk-free. The returns, too, are guaranteed by the Government. The funds in your account cannot be attached by even a court order to pay off debtors.

2. Multiple Tax Benefits:

PPF is an exempt-exempt-exempt (EEE) tax status scheme, presently the only investment in India to enjoy such an advantage. This makes it one of the most tax-efficient investments.

3. Small Savings, Good Returns:

The PPF allows you a lot of flexibility in the investment amount. Every year, you can invest a minimum of Rs.500/- and a maximum of Rs.1,50,000/-. You can make these investments in a maximum of 12 installments or as a lump sum.

4. Partial Withdrawal and Loan Facility:

Although the PPF has a 15 year lock-in period, you have many options to make use of the funds in your account. You can take a loan (up to 25% of the balance available at the end of two years preceding the year in which you apply for the loan) between the third year and the sixth year. However, you must repay the loan in 36 months and the rate of interest is 2% higher than the interest you earn.

From the seventh year, you can make partial withdrawals from your account. However, one withdrawal is allowed during the financial year. Besides partial withdrawals, you can prematurely close your PPF account if you need the funds for severe medical treatment or higher education.

5. The flexibility of Tenure:

When your PPF account matures after 15 years, you have two options, withdraw the entire amount or extend the tenure in blocks of five years. I have met many friends who told me that they were advised that the PPF account can be extended only once and they withdrew the money. Please note that this account can be extended for any number of years in a block of 5 years that too with "Contributions" or "without contributions" i.e. you may continue to make fresh deposits in your PPF account after 15 years or you may keep the account running without contributions also.

PPF Account Opening Rules:

The main rules of the PPF scheme are as under:

1. Eligibility Criteria:

- Only Indian Residents are allowed to invest in the scheme.
- A joint account cannot be opened.
- Parents can open a PPF account on behalf of a minor.
- In case both the parents are dead, grandparents can open a PPF account on behalf of their grandchildren.
- Only one account can be opened by an individual in his/her name.

Public Provident Fund

Calculation of Interest:
Currently, the rate of interest on the PPF account is 7.1% p.a. It may please be noted that the interest is calculated towards the scheme by the fifth of every month i.e. the calculation of interest is considered from the fifty days of the month to the last day of the month.

It is therefore advisable that individuals who are depositing lump sum amount in PPF account must try to make the payment by 5th April of every year. Calculation of interest is done on the monthly basis.

Tax Benefits:
Under Section 80C of the Income Tax Act, individuals can avail of tax benefits for the contribution made in the PPF account. As most of the senior citizens do not have much investment in tax saving schemes e.g. insurance, etc. they can avail of benefits up to Rs.1.50 lacs by investing in a PPF account where the interest generated from the contributions is also tax-exempt. Contributions made towards the PPF account are exempt from Wealth Tax as well.

Transfer of account:
PPF account from a post office can be transferred to a bank and vice versa. The PPF account can be transferred from one bank branch to another branch.

Power of Compounding:
I always prefer investment in PPF Account over any other investment not only for the reasons mentioned above but for the power of compounding it gives.

Let's understand it with some examples:

a) If an individual opens a PPF account at the age of 25 years and starts a deposit of only Rs. 5000/- per month for 35 years i.e. till he attains the retirement age, he will be getting approximately Rs. 90.79 lacs on maturity.

    The Sample calculations are as under:
    Total Investment @ 60,000/- p.a.   = 21.00 lacs
    Interest accrued @ 7.1% p.a.   = 69.79 lacs
    Total Maturity Value   = 90.79 lacs

b) If an individual opens a PPF account at the age of 25 years and starts a deposit of Rs. 10,000/- per month for 35 years i.e. till he retires, he will be getting approximately Rs. 181.58 lacs on maturity.

The Sample calculations are as under:
Total Investment @ 1,20,000/- p.a.	= 42.00 lacs
Interest accrued @ 7.1% p.a.	= 139.58 lacs
Total Maturity Value	= 181.58 lacs

c) Currently, the maximum contribution that can be made in the PPF account is Rs. 1.50 lacs per annum and if you deposit this amount every year for 30 years, you will be getting approximately Rs. 154.50 lacs at the age of 60 years as per the calculation below and if your spouse also opens the account and maintains it for the same duration, you will be getting a total amount of Rs.309.00 lacs which can be safely invested for taking care of your financial needs for rest of your life.

Total Investment @ 1,50,000/- p.a.	= 45.00 lacs
Interest accrued @ 7.1% p.a.	= 109.50 lacs
Total Maturity Value	= 154.50 lacs

d) However, I advise maintaining the PPF account even after the age of 60 also and making partial withdrawal every year for your monthly expenditure during the year. You will be able to meet your monthly expenditure for another 20-25 years depending upon your financial needs.

For Example, if you open a PPF account at the age of 35 and start depositing Rs.1,50,000/- p.a. up to the age of 80 years and start withdrawing Rs. 10,00,000/- p.a. from the age of 61 years for 20 years, you will still be left with around 26 lacs at the age of 81 years.

Suppose, you open two accounts i.e. for yourself and your spouse, you will be getting Rs.20,00,000/- per annum from which you will re-invest Rs.3,00,000/- in the PPF Account and still left with Rs. 17,00,000/- i.e. Rs.1,41,600/- per month for your household expenses. Moreover, this amount will be tax-free in your hands besides giving you tax benefit under section 80c of the Income Tax Act, if you are still in the Income Tax bracket as per current IT rules.

Going by the same calculations, if you open the PPF account at the age of 40 years, you still be getting Rs.7,00,000/- p.a. for another 20 years from 61 years of age leaving a balance of around Rs. 16 lacs in your hands at the age of 81 years.

However, if you open the PPF account at the age of 50 years and deposit Rs.1,50,000/- per annum, you will get Rs. 5,00,000/- p.a. from 66th year of your age for 15 years leaving a balance of approximately Rs. 17.50 lacs at the age of 81 years.

I have suggested many of my friends open the PPF account when they were approaching retirement at the age of 60 years. If you open the account at the age of 60 and start depositing Rs.1,50,000/- up to the age of 80 years, from the 71st year onward, you may get Rs. 4,00,000/- per annum leaving a balance of Rs. 6.60 lacs approximately at the age of 81 years.

Suppose, you open the account for your spouse also and he/she is also 60 years of age, you will get Rs. 8,00,000/- per annum and by depositing Rs. 3,00,000/- again, you will still be left with a tax-free income of Rs. 5,00,000/- per annum with approximately Rs. 13 lacs in your hands at the age of 81 years.

It looks a little awkward to talk of starting income from PPF account from the age of 61 years onwards but I can tell you from my experience that this investment of yours will give you confidence that will enhance your mental peace as you will always be confident that even if your savings will last for 10 years, what after that? The reply will be our PPF account.

Going by the age-old saying **"better late than never"**, open the PPF Account at the earliest and secure not only your future but you can also plan big expenses e.g. purchase of flat/house, car, etc. with these savings.

Let's summarize the pros-n-cons of PPF Account:

a) **Advantages:**

  i) PPF account is backed by the Central Government
  ii) It generates guaranteed returns
  iii) Flexible Investment Options
  iv) A very low investment scheme as you can deposit a minimum of Rs.500/- per year

v) The contribution made to PPF qualifies for rebate under Section 80C of the Income Tax Act.
vi) Interest earned on the PPF account is tax-free.
vii) The maturity proceeds are exempt from tax.
viii) PPF Accounts can be opened in the name of minors also.
ix) Loan facility available in PPF Account
x) Partial withdrawal facility available in PPF Account

b) **Disadvantages:**

i) It cannot be opened by HUF, NRIs, Trusts, etc.
ii) The big lock-in period of 15 years
iii) Lack of liquidity due to withdrawal restrictions
iv) There is a capping of the maximum contribution
v) Joint Account is not permitted in PPF
vi) Offers lower returns as compared to other investment avenues such as NPS, Mutual Fund, etc.
vii) Risk of inflation due to the fixed interest rate for a particular period.

14.
NATIONAL PENSION SCHEME

National Pension System – All Citizen Model (NPS) is a voluntary retirement scheme laid out to allow the subscribers to make a defined contribution towards planned savings thereby securing the future in the form of Pension.

At the time of normal exit from NPS, the subscribers may use the accumulated pension wealth under the scheme to purchase a life annuity from a Pension Fund Regulatory and Development Authority (PFRDA) impaneled life insurance company apart from withdrawing a part of accumulated pension wealth as lump-sum, if they choose so. PFRDA is the nodal agency for the implementation and monitoring of NPS.

A citizen of India, whether resident or non-resident can open an NPS account if he is within 18-65 years of age and should comply with KYC norms prescribed.

Benefits of NPS Account:

i) **Low Cost:**

NPS is considered to be the world's lowest-cost pension scheme. Administrative charges and fund management fees are also the lowest.

ii) **Simple:**

All applicant has to do is to open an account with any one of the POPs being run through all Head Posts Offices across the country and get a Permanent Retirement Account Number (PRAN).

iii) **Flexible:**

Applicants can choose /her investment option and Pension Fund or select an Auto choice to get better returns.

iv) Portable:

Applicant can operate an account from anywhere in the country and can pay contributions through any of the POP-SPs irrespective of the POP-SP branch with whom the applicant is registered, even if he/she changes his/her city, job, etc. and also make contributions through eNPS. The account can be shifted to any other sector like Government Sector, Corporate Model in case the subscriber gets employment.

e-NPS
Option I:

Any citizen of India, who meets the stipulated eligibility conditions can open his NPS account through an online facility –eNPS. With this facility, account holders can also make subsequent contributions to their account hassle-free using Net Banking / Debit Card / Credit Card.

Option II:

Entities called Point of Presence (POP) are appointed by PFRDA for servicing the individual subscribers, including their registration and acceptance of further contributions. The registration form for joining NPS can be collected from any of the Point of Presence – Service Providers (POP-SP). The subscriber can find the nearest POP-SP by clicking on https://npscra.nsdl.co.in/pop-sp.php.

To enroll under Central Government / State Government Sector, you may approach your HR Department / Pay and Accounts Office (the Nodal Office for NPS).

Tax Benefit:

Individuals who are employed and contributing to NPS would enjoy tax benefits on their contributions as well as their employers' contribution as under:

Employee's contribution:

Eligible for tax deduction up to 10% of salary (Basic+DA) under Section 80 CCD(1) within the overall ceiling of Rs. 1.50 lacs under Section 80 CCE.

Employer's Contribution:

The employee is eligible for tax deduction up to 10% of salary (Basic+DA) under Section 80 CCD(2) over and above the limit of Rs. 1.50 lacs provided under Section 80 CCE.

Self-employed:

Self-employed individuals are also eligible for tax deduction up to 10% of gross income under Section 80 CCD (1) within the overall ceiling of Rs. 1.50 lacs under Section 80 CCE. Subscriber is allowed a deduction in addition to the deduction allowed under Section 80 CCD (1) for additional contribution in his NPS account subject to a maximum investment of Rs. 50,000/- under Section 80 CCD (1B).

*Please note that tax benefits would be applicable as per the Income Tax Act, 1961 as amended from time to time.

Types of Accounts:

Tier – I Account:

The applicant shall contribute his/her savings for retirement into this condition; restricted withdrawal account. This is the retirement account and the applicant can claim tax benefits against the contributions made subject to the Income Tax Rules in force.

Tier – II Account:

This is a voluntary savings facility. The applicant will be free to withdraw his/her savings from this account whenever he/she wishes. This is not a retirement account and the applicant can't claim any tax benefits against contributions to this account.

Contributions:

The subscriber can contribute the amount through cash, cheque, demand draft, or Electronic Clearing System (ECS) at his/her chosen POP-SP. However, for cash transactions exceeding Rs. 50,000/- subscriber needs to submit a copy of the PAN Card. Please note no outstation cheques are accepted as a contribution.

Minimum Contributions (Tier-I)

- Minimum contribution at the time of account opening and for all subsequent transactions is Rs. 500/-
- Minimum Contribution per year – Rs.1,000/- excluding charges and taxes.
- The minimum number of contributions in a year is one.
- There is no maximum limit for contribution.

However, you can claim any additional self contribution (up to Rs.50,000/- under Section 80CCD(1b) as an NPS Tax benefit. The scheme, therefore, allows a tax deduction of up to Rs. 2 lacs in total.

Penalty for non-compliance of mandatory minimum contributions:

If the subscriber contributes less than Rs.1,000 in a year, his/her account would be frozen. To reactivate the account, the subscriber would have to pay the minimum contribution of Rs.500. However, a frozen account shall be closed when the account value falls to zero.

Minimum Contributions (Tier-II)

Minimum contribution at the time of account opening shall be Rs.1000/- and for all subsequent transactions a minimum amount per contribution is Rs.250/-. In Tier-II, there is no minimum contribution requirement for the financial year and also there is no cap on maximum contribution.

How to open an NPS Account:

As a subscriber between the age of 18 to 65 years of age, you can procure your Permanent Retirement Account Number (PRAN) from any of the POP-SP you wish to register with.

You can also join NPS Online and the steps to be followed are as under:

1. You must have a Permanent Account Number (PAN)
2. Bank / Demat / Folio account details with the impaneled Bank/ Non-Bank for KYC verification for subscriber registration through e-NPS.
3. Your KYC verification will be done by the Bank / Non-Bank POP selected by you during the registration process. The name and address provided during registration should match with POP records for KYC verification. If the details don't match, the request is liable for rejection. In case of rejection of KYC by the selected POP, the applicant is requested to contact the POP.
4. You need to fill up all the mandatory details online.
5. You need to upload a scanned copy of the PAN Card and canceled cheque in the prescribed format file size between 4KB-2MB.

6. You need to upload your scanned photograph and signature in *.jpeg/*.jpg/*.png format having a file size between 4KB-5MB.
7. You will be routed to a payment gateway for making the payment towards your NPS account from Internet Banking.
8. Contributions are credited in PRAN on a T+2 basis (subject to receipt of clear funds from Payment Gateway Service Provider).

After the Permanent Retirement Account Number (PRAN) is allotted, the subscriber can use the following options:

Option 1 – e-Sign

1. Select the "e-sign" option on the e-sign/Print and courier page.
2. OTP for authentication will be sent to your mobile number registered with the Aadhaar.
3. After authentication of Aadhaar, Registration will be successfully e-signed.
4. Once a document is e-signed, you need not send the physical copy of the form to Central Record Keeping Agency (CRA). PFRDA has appointed NSDL and KARVY as CRA for NPS. Both ventures in India carry out the functions of record-keeping, administration, and customer service for all subscribers under NPS.
5. e-Sign service charges plus taxes applicable is Rs. 25.90 (including UIDAI charges of Rs. 20/-)

Option 2 – Print and Courier

1. Select the 'Print and Courier' option on the e-sign/print & courier page.
2. You need to take a printout of the form, paste your photograph (please do not sign across the photograph), and affix your signature.
3. You should sign on the block provided for signature.
4. The photograph should not be stapled or clipped to the form.
5. The form should be sent within 30 days from the date of allotment of PRAN to CRA at the following address or else the PRAN will be 'frozen' temporarily.

Central Recordkeeping Agency (e-NPS)
NSDL e-Governance Infrastructure Limited,
1st Floor, Times Tower, Kamala Mills Compound,
Senapati Bapat Marg,
Lower Parel, Mumbai-400 013.

(For queries, you may write to:eNPS@nsdl.co.in)
The list of POP-SP (Service Provider branches) is available on the CRA website www.nspcra.nsdl.co.in and on the website of the concerned POP. To know the nearest POP-SP branch of your choice, you may visit https://www.npscra.nsdl.co.in/pop-sp.php.

After the account is opened, CRA shall mail a "Welcome Kit" containing the subscriber's unique Permanent Retirement Account Number (PRAN) Card and the complete information provided by the subscriber. This account number will be the primary means of identifying and operating the account. You will also receive a Telephone Password (TPIN) which can be used to access an account on the call center number (1-800-222080). You will also be provided an Internet Password (IPIN) for accessing an account on the CRA Website (www.npscra.nsdl.co.in) on a 24x7 basis.

Investment Options:

Under NPS, how the money is invested will depend upon your own choice. NPS offers several funds and multiple investment options to choose from. In case you do not want to exercise a choice, your money will be invested as per the Default choice of "Moderate Life Cycle Fund" under the "Auto Choice" option. In the auto choice, option money will get invested in various types of schemes as per your age. The NPS offers two approaches to investing your money.

Active Choice:

You will have the option to actively decide as to how your NPS pension wealth is to be invested in the following three options:

Asset Class E:

Investments in predominantly in equity market instruments.

Asset Class C:

Investments in fixed income instruments other than the government securities

Asset Class G:

Investments in Government securities

Asset Class A:

Investment in Alternative Investment Schemes including instruments like Commercial Mortgage-Backed Securities (CMBS), Mortgage-Backed Securities (MBS), Real Estate Investment Trusts (REITs), Infrastructure Investment Trusts (InvIts), etc

You can choose to invest entire pension wealth in C or G asset classes and up to a maximum of 50% in equity (Asset Class E) and up to a maximum of 5% in 'Asset Class A'. You can also distribute your pension wealth across E, C, G, and A Asset Classes, subject to such conditions as may be prescribed by PFRDA.

Auto Choice – Lifecycle Fund

NPS offers an easy option to manage your investments. In case you are unable/unwilling to exercise any choice as regards asset allocation, your funds will be invested by the Auto Choice option. In this option, the investments will be made in a life-cycle fund. Here, the proportion of funds invested across three asset classes will be determined by a pre-defined portfolio (which would change as per age of subscriber), with the investment in E decreasing and in C & G increasing with the age of the subscriber. Three Life Cycle Funds are available under this Auto Choice:

(i) LC75 – Aggressive Life Cycle Fund

In this fund, the exposure in Equity Investments starts with 75% till age 35 and gradually reduces as per the age of the subscriber.

(ii) LC50 – Moderate Life Cycle Fund:

In this fund, the exposure in Equity Investments starts with 50% till age 35 and gradually reduces as per the age of the subscriber.

(iii) LC 25 – Conservative Life Cycle Fund:

In this fund, the exposure in Equity Investments starts with 25% till age 35 and gradually reduces as per the age of the subscriber.

However, the default auto choice is if the subscriber is not choosing any of the above options if Moderate Life Cycle Fund.

Withdrawal / Exit:

1. Upon attainment of the age of 60 years:

At least 40% of the accumulated pension wealth needs to be utilized for purchase of annuity providing for monthly pension to the subscriber and balance is paid as lump sum payment. In case the total accumulated corpus is less than Rs.2 lacs, the subscriber may opt for a 100% lump-sum withdrawal.

However, you have the option to defer the lump sum withdrawal till the age of 70 years. You have also got the option to continue contributing up to the age of 70 years. This option is required to be exercised up to 15 days before the completion of 60 years.

2. At any time before attaining the age of 60 years:

You may exit from NPS before attaining the age of 60 years, only if he has completed 10 years in NPS. At least 80% of the accumulated pension wealth of the subscriber needs to be utilized for the purchase of annuity providing for monthly pension and the balance is paid as a lump sum payment to the subscriber. If the total corpus is less than Rs. 1 lac, you may opt for a 100% lump-sum withdrawal.

3. Death of the Subscriber:

In such an unfortunate event, an option will be available to the nominee to receive 100% of the NPS pension wealth in a lump sum. However, if the nominee wishes to continue with NPS, he/she shall have to subscribe to NPS individually after following the due procedure under National Pension System.

Let's summarize the pros-n-cons of the National Pension Scheme:

a. Advantages:

i) Low Investment
ii) Higher Returns
iii) Wide Coverage and bigger canvas
iv) Regulations that safeguard the investment
v) Easy Access
vi) A very cheap plan
vii) Easy Maintenance of the Account

viii) Multiple investment options
ix) Funds invested by the able Fund Managers & option to change the Fund Manager

b. Disadvantages:

i) Withdrawal Limitations
ii) Taxation at the time of withdrawal
iii) Investment Restrictions
iv) Account Opening Restrictions
v) No Guaranteed Returns

15.
POST OFFICE SCHEMES

Currently, for small savings various Post office saving schemes are the best option as the interest being offered in these schemes are comparatively higher than any other scheme. Moreover, investments in Post Office are the least risk investments.

However, whenever I was discussing these schemes in my Financial Planning sessions, many of my friends were hesitant to go for PO savings because of the bureaucratic setup of Post Offices and maybe their experience.

Now, most of the Post Offices have been computerized and their services are at par with banks or maybe better. If you go with my experience, I have always found the Post Office personnel very helpful and cooperative.

There are many schemes available to take care of the short-term/long-term needs of individuals. Let's discuss these schemes:

15.1 KISAN VIKAS PATRA (KVP)

If you are looking for a long term investment, KVP is the second-best option after PPF. You can invest any amount from a minimum of Rs. 1,000/- for a long term and you will be earning 6.9% interest (applicable from 1.4.2020 till December 2021) p.a. compounded annually for 124 months (10 years and 4 months) when the amount invested will be doubled. Although this scheme is for 124 months, you can withdraw the amount along with applicable interest after 30 months.

KVP account may be opened by an individual singly or jointly (up to 3 adults) or even by a minor in his name if he is above 10 years. Further, any number of accounts can be opened under this scheme.

KVP may be pledged or transferred as security, for taking a loan from Banks/Corporations/Housing Finance companies, etc.

This account is beneficial if you are planning to achieve long term goals. Suppose you plan to purchase a flat after 10 years by availing loan from Bank/Financial Institution but are worried about EMIs. Start investing surplus money available at your disposal after meeting your monthly expenses/liabilities and you will find that part of your EMIs shall be taken care of every month from these KVPs, you purchased regularly from your surplus funds.

Let's summarize the pros-n-cons of KVP:

a) Advantages:

i) It is a Central Government scheme with guaranteed returns without any risk.
ii) No higher ceiling limit for investment in KVP with a minimum investment fixed at Rs.100/-
iii) KVP is more liquid as compared to NSC, PPF, NPS as withdrawal is permitted after two-and-a-half years of investment.
iv) KVP can be used as collateral security for a loan from Banks.
v) No TDS is deducted in this scheme.
vi) Offers a higher rate of interest as compared to bank Fixed Deposits.
vii) Higher returns on investment due to compounding of the interest.

b) Disadvantages:

i) This scheme is not eligible for tax benefits under Section 80C.
ii) NRIs and HUFs are not eligible to purchase KVP.
iii) KVP's lock-in period is somewhat on the higher side as compared to the usual Fixed Deposits that can be broken at any time with a small penalty.
iv) No cash payments are allowed at the time of withdrawal.

15.2 NATIONAL SAVINGS CERTIFICATE (NSC)

One of the most popular saving schemes of Post Office is NSC (VIII issue). Currently (from 1.4.2020 till December 2021), it offers an interest rate of 6.8% p.a. compounded annually but payable at maturity i.e. 5 years from the date of opening of the account. An investment made under this scheme qualifies for deduction under Section 80C of the Income Tax Act, which makes this scheme even more attractive. Even, the interest earned on NSC also qualifies as a deduction under Section 80C of the IT Act (except in the last year of the instrument's tenure).

Other terms and conditions of the opening of the NSC account are similar to the KVP account as mentioned above. However, unlike KVP, NSC can't be prematurely closed except under some exceptional circumstances.

Let's summarize the pros-n-cons of the NSC account:

a) **Advantages:**

   i) It is a risk-free investment being a government scheme.
   ii) Interest earned gets compounded annually and reinvested by default, payable on maturity.
   iii) The rate of interest is comparatively higher than bank fixed deposits.
   iv) The investment and interest which is re-invested are eligible for deduction under Section 80C of the IT Act.
   v) NSCs can be used as collateral security for a loan from banks.
   vi) There is no TDS on NSC payouts.
   vii) Joint Account and nomination facility available in NSC.

b) **Disadvantages:**

   i) NSC is not redeemable before its maturity except under some exceptional situations.
   ii) In the NSC VIII issue, funds are locked for 5 years.
   iii) The interest earned in the 5th year is not re-invested hence taxable as per the investor's applicable slab rates.

15.3 SUKANYA SAMRIDHI SCHEME

The Sukanya Samriddhi Yojana (SSY) is a government-backed small deposit scheme for a girl child and her financial needs. An SSY account can be opened any time after the birth of a girl's child till she turns 10 with a minimum deposit of Rs.250/- only. In subsequent years, a minimum of Rs.250 and a maximum of Rs. 1.50 lacs can be deposited during the ongoing financial year.

The account will remain operative for 21 years from the date of its opening or till the marriage of the girl after she turns 18 (1 month before or 3 months after marriage). For a child's higher education expenses, withdrawal of 50% of the balance is allowed after the girl child turns 18.

Only one account in the name of the girl child can be opened by parents or guardians with a notified bank or post office in the name of the girl. A birth certificate of the girl child along with residence proof & Identity proof of depositor is also required for opening the account.

To keep the account active, a minimum contribution of Rs.250 is mandatory in each financial year (and in multiples of Rs.100 thereafter and maximum Rs. 1.5 lacs up to the end of the 15th year from the opening of the account.

The SSY enjoys an exempt-exempt-exempt (EEE) status. The annual contribution qualifies for Section 80C and the maturity benefits are non-taxable.

SSY being a government-backed small saving scheme, the interest rates are decided by the government every quarter. From 1.4.2020 (till December 2021) the interest rate on the SSY scheme is 7.6% p.a. calculated on yearly basis, yearly compounded.

SSY account can be transferred anywhere in India if the girl child in whose name the account has been opened shifts to another place on furnishing proof of shifting of residence of either the parent/guardian or account holder.

Let's summarize the pros-n-cons of the SSY Scheme:

a) **Advantages:**

   i) SSY has a tax-exempt status at all stages of investment.

ii) Being a Central Government sponsored scheme, it guarantees the safety of your Principal and Interest.
iii) The interest amount though not fixed will be in line with the general investment scenario.
iv) SSY scheme allows by default of building of the investment discipline because of Illiquidity.
v) It offers attractive interest rates in the present scenario.

b) **Disadvantages:**

i) The amount deposited under this account matures only after the 21st year of deposit.
ii) SSY scheme allows only two accounts per family.
iii) There is an upper cap on investment.
iv) The opportunity is lost for girls who have crossed 10 years of age.
v) Currently, there is no provision for operating an SSY account online.

15.4 MONTHLY INCOME SCHEME ACCOUNT (MIS)

Post Office Monthly Income Scheme is a highly reliable, low-risk scheme and generates a steady income with a primary objective of capital protection. The MIS account can be opened with a minimum investment of Rs.1000/- and a maximum of up to Rs. 4.50 lacs individually or up to Rs. 9.0 lacs jointly with an equal share of all account holders.

Being a government-backed savings scheme, interest is decided every quarter. However, the interest rates remain firm for the entire period of the scheme as applicable on the date of opening of the account. From 1.4.2020 till December 2021, the current interest rates are 6.6% p.a. payable monthly.

This scheme has a maturity period of 5 years. The interest received on monthly basis can be transferred to your savings account or Recurring Deposit account as per your Standing instructions.

This scheme is particularly beneficial if the monthly income received from MIS has invested again in a Systematic Investment Plan (SIP) to generate higher returns. An investment made under MIS Scheme is not covered under Section 80C, however, no TDS is deducted.

This is a favourable scheme for senior citizens as they can deposit their life savings in the MIS account guarantying the highest safety for their capital invested and earning interest for their monthly expenses.

Let's summarize the pros-n-cons of MIS Account:

a) **Advantages:**

  i) Being a Government of India product, it is one of the safest investments.
  ii) As a fixed income scheme, investment is not subject to market risks/volatility.
  iii) It is a source of regular income after retirement.
  iv) MIS Account does not have TDS.
  v) It allows premature withdrawal also.

vi) It can also be renewed for a further period of 5 years.
vii) You can move the monthly payouts to the RD Account.
viii) You can open a joint account with 2 or 3 people.

b) Disadvantages:

i) There is a ceiling of maximum investment for individuals.
ii) Interest income from this scheme is taxable in your hands.
iii) If the monthly payouts are not withdrawn, they do not earn any interest.
iv) Investment in the name of a minor cannot exceed Rs.3 lacs.

15.5 TIME DEPOSIT ACCOUNT (TD)

Under a small savings scheme, Post Office offers a time deposit or National Savings Time Deposit Account (TD). It is almost similar to a bank's fixed deposit.

Any individual above the age of 10 can open a time deposit account at any post office. Further, guardians can open an account on behalf of a minor. Accounts can also be held jointly by up to 3 individuals. Depositors can also nominate a person before or after opening an account.

One of the primary benefits of a time deposit is that individuals can create multiple accounts without any restriction. Depositors also have the freedom to transfer their accounts from one post office to another.

Time Deposit accounts can be opened for multiple lock-in periods i.e. 1, 2, 3 & 5 years. Moreover, account tenure can be extended by giving a formal application. The minimum amount required to open a Time Deposit Account is Rs.1,000/-. Individuals can deposit in multiples of Rs.100 thereof and there is no limit for maximum investment.

For a 5-year time deposit account, depositors will be able to claim income tax exemptions of up to Rs. 1.50 lakh under Section 80C of the Income Tax Act, 1961.

The rates of interest applicable on Time Deposit Account are comparatively higher than the Fixed Deposit interest rates being offered by various banks as of date.

The post office term deposit interest rate is revised every quarter by the Government of India. The interest is calculated quarterly and paid annually. From September 2020, the interest rates are as under:-

Tenure 1, 2 & 3 year	-	5.5%
Tenure 5 year	-	6.7%

Just for comparison purposes let's look at the interest rates on fixed deposits being offered by the State Bank of India, which is 5% for 1 year FD and 5.40% for 5 years Fixed Deposit from November 2021 for the general public.

Let's summarize the pros-n-cons of Post Office Time Deposit:

a) Advantages:

i) The minimum amount to open a POTD account is Rs.1000 and there is no maximum limit. You can convert your account from a single to a joint account and vice versa.

ii) The capital in the POTD is completely protected with guaranteed returns, being a Government-backed account.

iii) The POTD is liquid, despite the deposit lock-in, you can borrow against the deposit or withdraw the deposit prematurely.

iv) You can claim income tax deduction under Section 80C of the Income Tax Act on the deposit made in the 5 year Time Deposit Account.

b) Disadvantages:

i) If the interest earned exceeds Rs.40,000 per financial year for regular customers, the tax may be deducted at source by the Post Office.

ii) Maturity proceeds not drawn are eligible to savings account interest rate for a maximum period of two years.

iii) The POTD is not inflation protected, which means whenever inflation is above the guaranteed interest rate, the return from the scheme earns no real returns.

16.
SENIOR CITIZEN SAVINGS SCHEME

The Senior Citizens Savings Scheme (SCSS) was launched with the main aim of providing Indian Citizens with a regular income after they attain the retirement age i.e. 60 years or above. However, Defence services personnel are eligible irrespective of their age for fulfilling certain other conditions and individuals who have attained the age of 55 years old, but are below the age of 60 years and have retired on superannuation are also eligible. This scheme is open only for Indian individuals i.e. Non-Resident Indians (NRI) and Hindu Undivided Families (HUF) are not eligible to open an SCSS. This scheme is available at Post Offices and certified banks across the country i.e. most of the nationalized banks are offering SCSS schemes.

The main features of the SCSS are as under:-

1. Although the current interest rate in SCSS is 7.40% p.a., it is still high when compared to other savings and Fixed Deposit options. In the first instance, the interest is payable on the deposit date of March 31, September 30 and December 31st. Thereafter, interest is paid at quarterly intervals on the initial working day of April, July, October and December 31.
2. The maturity period of the scheme is 5 years. Maturity can be extended for another 3 years by applying within one year of maturity of the account. Moreover, premature withdrawal is allowed after one year from the date of opening the account. However, a charge of 1.5% will be levied for premature withdrawal after one year and a charge of 1% shall be levied for premature withdrawal after 2 years.

3. Individuals are allowed to operate more than one account by themselves or open a joint account with their spouse only. In the case of a joint account, the initial depositor is the investor of the joint account. It means you can open two joint accounts also i.e. Husband & Wife and Wife & Husband, provided you both fulfil other conditions and eligibility criteria. Moreover, nominations can be added to the scheme at the time of opening an account or after the account has been opened.
4. Only a single deposit is allowed to be made in the account and it has to be in the multiples of Rs.1000 and the maximum amount that can be deposited is Rs. 15 lakh.
5. Under Section 80C of the Income Tax Act, individuals are eligible for tax deductions on investment up to Rs. 1.50 lakh. In case the interest generated is more than Rs.10,000/- p.a., the tax will be deducted at the source.

Opening an SCSS Account is a hassle-free process. Visit the nearest certified bank or post office with the following documents:-

1. Self-attested copy of the PAN Card
2. Self-attested copy of the Adhaar Card
3. Two passport-size photographs (in case of a joint account, a single passport size photo of both husband & wife is generally asked for)
4. Duly filled in Form A (The form is available with bank/post office)
5. A cheque for the amount that is being deposited. (The account opening date shall be the date of realization of the cheque)

Let's summarize the pros-n-cons of SCSS:

a) **Advantages:**

   i) SCSS being a government-sponsored scheme is one of the safest investment options for senior citizens.
   ii) If both husband and wife are above 60 years of age, both are eligible to open SCSS accounts either individually or jointly.
   iii) Once an account holder locks the interest rate, it remains the same till the maturity of the scheme. This protects the account holders from decreasing interest rates.

iv) Quarterly payment is made under the scheme which is beneficial for retirees and others who may need fixed income to meet their regular expenditure.
v) There is an option to renew the account after maturity i.e. 5 years.
vi) There is an option of premature withdrawal after one year of opening the account. Further, there is no penalty if the account holder closes the account after renewing it post completion of five years.
vii) An individual can open more than one SCSS account by opting for a joint account with his/her spouse.

b) Disadvantages:

i) An individual is not allowed to invest more than Rs.15 lakhs in the account.
ii) Quarterly payouts may be unnecessary for people who are not looking for a fixed income as it deprives the individual of earning higher returns due to the power of compounding.
iii) Premature withdrawals carry a penalty.
iv) The interest income is subjected to tax deducted at the source. This may be very inconvenient as a senior citizen has to file a tax return to get the excess TDS even if they do not have a taxable income.

17.
PRADHAN MANTRI VAYA VANDANA YOJANA

Pradhan Mantri Vaya Vandana Yojana (PMVVY) is a retirement cum pension scheme that was launched in May 2017 by the Government of India. It offers an assured rate of return on investment. In the current low-interest-rate scenario, senior citizens are finding it difficult to renew their fixed deposits posing problems for them if they rely on interest income to meet their regular household expenses.

The PMVVY scheme was extended by the Government multiple times until March 31, 2020. The scheme has been further extended until March 31, 2023, but with some important changes to the original scheme. The scheme is managed solely by the Life Insurance Corporation of India (LIC). Under the modified scheme, Government will decide the interest rate every year, for the FY 2021 the interest rate has been fixed at 7.4% p.a. Thus, for the next year, the interest rate may be different but for those who purchase the scheme till 31st March 2022, the interest rate will remain fixed at 7.4% p.a. for the entire duration of the scheme i.e. for 10 years. It is just like a bank fixed deposit or a Senior Citizen Savings Scheme, where the interest rate is locked until maturity. Additionally, the Government has specified that the interest rate for PMVVY will be along the lines of SCSS (the current interest rate for the Senior Citizen Savings Scheme is also 7.4%).

PMVVY Scheme is only for senior citizens who are 60 years of age and above. It is a pension scheme that comes with guaranteed returns on a monthly, quarterly, half-yearly or annual basis for 10 years. The maximum investment that can be made in the scheme is restricted to

Rs. 15 lakh per senior citizen and the maximum monthly pension in the scheme is Rs.9,250/- per senior citizen. Therefore, if both spouses are above the age of 60 years, the maximum monthly pension can be Rs.18,500/- in the family on investment of Rs.30 lakhs. However, it may please be noted that the pension in PMVVY is not dependent on the age of the investor.

Salient Features of Pradhan Mantri Vaya Vandana Yojana (PMVVY):

1. Minimum Entry Age: 60 years
2. Maximum Entry Age: No Limit
3. Policy Term   10 years
4. Minimum Pension: Rs. 1,000/- per month or Rs.12,000/- p.a.
5. Maximum Pension: Rs.9,250/- per month or Rs.1,11,000/- p.a.

Mode of Pension	Minimum Purchase Price (Rs.)	Minimum Pension (Rs.)	Maximum Purchase Price (Rs.)	Maximum Pension (Rs.)
Yearly	1,56,658	12000	14,49,086	1,11,000
Half-Yearly	1,59,574	6000	14,76,064	55,500
Quarterly	1,61,074	3000	14,89,933	27,750
Monthly	1,62,162	1000	15,00,000	9,250

6. The limit on maximum investment is per senior citizen. Therefore, if your spouse is also a senior citizen, the maximum investment in the scheme can be Rs. 30 lakhs.
7. The scheme is exempt from Goods and Services Tax (GST)
8. The Government has declared the interest rate of 7.4% payable monthly i.e. 7.66% per annum for the entire duration of 10 years.
9. Unlike other pension plans, the amount of pension is not dependent on age.
10. The loan facility is available after the completion of 3 policy years. The maximum loan that can be granted shall be 75% of the Purchase Price. The rate of interest to be charged for a loan amount is determined at periodic intervals.
11. In the event of the death of the policyholder during the policy term of 10 years, the purchase price shall be returned to the beneficiary. In the event of survival till maturity, the purchase price along with the final pension instalment shall be paid on maturity.

12. The premature exit is allowed only if the pensioner needs money for the treatment of any terminal/critical illness of self or spouse with a premature exit penalty of 2%.
13. There is no tax benefit for investment in PMVVY. Pension will be taxed at your marginal income tax rate. However, there is no tax charged when the purchase price is returned at the time of maturity or death.
14. The pension payment shall be through NEFT or Aadhaar Enabled Payment System. The Purchase of the policy under this scheme requires unique Aadhaar number validation.
15. This scheme can be purchased offline as well as online. To purchase this scheme online, you have to log in to the LIC website www.licindia.in.

Let's summarize the pros-n-cons of the PMVVY Scheme:

a) **Advantages:**

   i) PMVVY is a simple and easy to understand product with the highest safety of capital.
   ii) The scheme offers a much better interest rate than any other such investment in the present interest rate scenario.
   iii) The interest rates are locked for 10 years.
   iv) As purchase price does not depend on age, it is good for those senior citizens who are in their early sixties as the annuity rates, even for without return of purchase price variant, are likely to be lower than PMVVY interest rate.
   v) The scheme offers a pension at regular intervals as per your choice.

b) **Disadvantages:**

   i) The scheme lacks in terms of tax-efficient as no tax-saving benefit comes with other pension schemes like NPS, SCSS, etc.
   ii) PMVVY has a long lock-in period of 10 years, so 'liquidity can be a factor as you cannot access money except in case of serious illness.
   iii) There is a maximum investment limit of Rs.15 lacs per senior citizen. Therefore, the quantum of income from this scheme is capped.
   iv) PMVVY is not an annuity product where the interest rate is locked for life. After maturity i.e. 10 years, you have to look for a similar plan to manage your regular income.

18.
DEPOSIT INSURANCE & CREDIT GUARANTE CORPORATION

Deposit Insurance & Credit Guarantee Corporation (DICGC) insures all deposits such as savings, fixed, current, recurring deposits, etc. deposited in all commercial banks including branches of foreign banks functioning in India, local area banks and regional rural banks.

Each depositor in a bank is insured up to Rs. 5,00,000/- (Rupees Five Lac) for both principal and interest amount held by him in the same right and same capacity as on the date of liquidation/cancellation of bank's licence or the date on which the scheme of amalgamation/merger/reconstruction comes into force. All funds held in the same type of ownership at the same bank (including different branches) are added together before deposit insurance is determined. However, if the funds are in different types of ownership or are deposited into separate banks they would then be separately insured.

If more than one deposit account is jointly held by individuals in one or more branches of a bank, say three individuals X, Y & Z hold more than one joint deposit accounts in which their names appear in the same order then all these accounts are considered as held in the same capacity and the same right. Accordingly, balances held in all these accounts will be aggregated to determine the insured amount within the limit of Rs.5 lakhs. However, if individuals open more than one joint accounts in which their names are not in the same order, for example, X, Y & Z; Z, Y & X and Y, X & Z or a group of persons are different say X, Y & Z and X, Y & A etc.

then, the deposits held in these joint accounts are considered as held in the different capacity and different right. Accordingly, insurance cover will be available separately up to Rs. 5 lakh to every such joint account where the names appearing in different order or names are different.

If a bank goes into liquidation, DICGC is liable to pay to the liquidator the claim amount of each depositor up to Rs. 5 lakh within two months from the date of receipt of the claim list from the liquidator. The liquidator has to disburse the claim amount to each insured depositor corresponding to their claim amount. If a bank is reconstructed or amalgamated/merged with another bank, the DICGC pays the bank concerned, the difference between the full amount of deposit or the limit of insurance cover in force at the time, whichever is less and the amount received by him under the reconstruction/amalgamation scheme within two months from the date of receipt of claim list from the transferee bank/CEO of the insured bank/transferee bank as the case may be.

Please note that DICGC never deals directly with the depositors of the failed bank. In the event of a bank's liquidation, the liquidator prepares a depositor wise claim list and sends it to the DICGC for scrutiny and payment. However, the DICGC pays the money to the liquidator who is liable to pay the depositors. In the case of amalgamation/merger of banks, the amount due to each depositor is paid to the transferee bank.

The Corporation may cancel the registration of an insured bank if it fails to pay the premium for three consecutive periods. In the event of the DICGC withdrawing its coverage from any bank for default in the payment of premium, the public will be notified through newspapers. Registration of an insured bank stands cancelled if the bank is prohibited from receiving fresh deposits, or its licence is cancelled or a licence is refused to it by the RBI, or it is would up either voluntarily or compulsorily; or it ceases to be a banking company or a co-operative bank, etc. However, in the event of the cancellation of registration of a bank, deposits of the bank remain covered by the insurance till the date of the cancellation.

The DICGC has deposit insurance liability on liquidation etc. of "Insured Banks" i.e. banks that have been de-registered:

(a) On account of a prohibition on receiving fresh deposits
(b) On cancellation of licence or it is found that licence cannot be granted.

On liquidation etc. of other de-registered banks i.e. banks which have been de-registered on other grounds such as non-payment of premium or their ceasing to be eligible co-operative banks, the Corporation will have no liability.

19.
FIXED DEPOSITS

A fixed deposit in the bank is one of the most popular investment options in India and several people in our country invest a significant portion of their savings in this instrument.

A fixed deposit is a financial instrument in which there is a fixed rate of interest for a fixed period. Tenure of deposit can range from as little as 7 days and it can be up to 10 years. In this investment, a sum of money is locked for a fixed period. There is very low risk involved while the returns are guaranteed as they are free from stock market volatility. Thus, it is an ideal choice for those who are less aware of the capital market.

One of the reasons for the popularity of fixed deposit is that it is a liquid option. Depositors have a sense of security that in case of any emergency/exigency, they may break the FD prematurely and get instant money to mitigate the emergency. The penalty for premature withdrawal of FD is minimal when compared to an emergency. Moreover, the bank fixed deposits are backed with an insurance of Rs. 5 lakh (principal & interest) by DICGC as explained above.

Different banks offer fixed deposits at a different rate of interest which is published on their website and they offer a higher rate of interest for Senior Citizens ranging generally up to 0.50% more than regular interest rates. All the banks provide their customers with tax-saving FD options up to Rs. 1.5 lakh which can be quoted in deductions u/s 80C of the IT Act. However, these schemes come with a lock-in period of 5 years where no premature withdrawals are allowed.

All banks offer payment of interest in two ways, viz. Cumulative and Non-cumulative. In the cumulative option, interest is paid on maturity along with the principal and it offers the compounding effect as already explained as most of the banks pay interest every quarter which gets added to the principal amount, thus resulting in a higher payout on maturity. However, for persons looking for regular income, banks offer a non-cumulative option where the interest is paid on a quarterly, half-yearly and annual basis as decided by the investor. Though it depends upon the choice of the investor, it is advisable to go for the cumulative option to earn maximum returns by letting the power of compounding work. Opening a fixed deposit is very simple and can be done offline or online.

Now a day, many small finance banks are offering comparatively higher interest rates than established banks. To take advantage of higher interest rates, you may go for Fixed Deposits with these banks but keep a limit so that the principal and interest is within the threshold limit of Rs.5 lakh for which insurance cover is provided by DICGC. However, if you have limited options for such small banks in your area, you may consider opening joint accounts and ensuring that the names are in a different order in such accounts so that they are separately covered for DICGC insurance.

As the interest rates are at their lowest during present times, it is better to open Fixed Deposit with different durations e.g. 1 year, 2 years, 3 years, etc. so that you can reap the benefit of higher interest rates in future on the maturity of these fixed deposits if you wish to continue with fixed deposits.

Further, it is advisable to open multiple FDs even if you have to open them on the same date and for the same duration. Let's say, you plan to open an FD of Rs. 5 lakh for 3 years, better is to open 3 FDs for 2 lakh, 2 lakh & 1 lakh. It will give more liquidity in your hands as in case of any emergency/exigency, you may break the FD for the amount required instead of breaking full FD and losing interest.

Let's summarize the pros-n-cons of Fixed Deposits:

a) **Advantages:**

  i) Fixed Deposits are safe and offer an assured rate of return.
  ii) The tenure for a fixed deposit is flexible and depends on the investor.

iii) It is relatively easy to liquidate a fixed deposit. For FDs booked online, they can be liquidated online via net banking as well.
iv) Taking a loan against FD is very easy and banks offer loans up to 95% of the FD amount depending upon the bank.
v) No TDS is deducted by banks on any interest paid until it crosses the threshold limit of Rs.40,000/- for regular customers and Rs.50,000/- for Senior Citizens on different fixed deposits.

b) **Disadvantages:**

i) The interest rates do not move in line with inflation and may earn less than the inflation rate in some cases.
ii) The fixed deposits lock in your funds for a fixed duration.
iii) The interest earned on fixed deposits is taxable income beyond the threshold limit of Rs.40,000 (for Senior Citizens up to Rs.50,000/-) and TDS is deducted by banks.
iv) The rate of interest remains fixed for the entire duration of the FD and even if the rates increase, the bank does not pay additional interest to the deposit holder.
v) Premature withdrawal of FDs carries a penalty.

20.
COMPANY FIXED DEPOSITS

Fixed deposits in Companies are similar to fixed deposits in Banks and are for fixed terms carrying a prescribed rate of interest, which generally is a little better than bank deposits. The company fixed deposits are offered by Financial and Non-Banking Financial Companies (NBFC). The maturities of such deposits can range from a few months to a few years.

However, the main difference is that these deposits are not insured by DICGC. Therefore, it is advisable to remember the following points before investing in Company Fixed Deposits:

Check Credit Ratings:

It is a very important indicator about the health of the company highlighting the existing risk of the Company. Various agencies provide such credit ratings as ICRA, CRISIL, etc. For example, in the case of ratings by ICRA, you can read them as under:-

Highest Safety:
(Lowest risk of turning into a defaulter)　　　　ICRA AAA
High Safety:
(Very low credit risk)　　　　　　　　　　　　ICRA AA
Low Risk　　　　　　　　　　　　　　　　　　ICRA A
Moderate Safety:
(Moderate credit risk)　　　　　　　　　　　　ICRA BBB

It is advisable to invest in the Companies with Credit Rating "AAA" as it indicates that you can trust the company and expect it to pay the interest amount due on time with the security of your principal.

Check Promoter Credibility:

Promoters play an important role in making or breaking a company. Promoters with a doubtful past track record or those who lack sturdiness in records should be strictly avoided.

Beware of High-Interest Rate Offering Companies:

Any company offering a very high-interest rate should be a cause of concern because they offer a high rate of interest to make up for the perceived risk attached with their offerings. It holds true with any other investment also and you must be beware of such lucrative offers.

Seek the help of a Regulator:

There are regulators to keep a check on any frauds or mishandling of public money by companies like in mutual funds and stock exchanges. Therefore, in case the company in which you have invested defaults; check who is the regulator and complain about them e.g. SEBI for listed companies, RBI for banks and NBFCs, and DCA for manufacturing companies.

Spread your risk:

It is better to diversify your risk among various companies if you are investing in company Fixed Deposit and such companies should be working with a different types of industries. Further, depending upon the rate of interest and your time horizon, make such investments for 1 year to 5 years and decide whether you want regular returns or cumulative interest on maturity.

Let's summarize the pros-n-cons of Company FDs:

a) **Advantages:**

  i) Company deposits are carefully inspected by credit rating agencies. These agencies check whether such FDs are safe and stable. Therefore, these deposits are considered safe if the deposits are made in the company having 'AAA' ratings only.
  ii) Company Fixed Deposits generally offer higher interest rates as compared to Bank Deposits.

iii) Corporate FDs provide flexibility of tenor as you can invest in the company deposit for a tenor ranging from 12 to 60 months. Further, the interest rate payment is also flexible.
iv) Some companies offer added incentives to their customers when they renew their FDs. This allows extra income for them though slightly.

b) Disadvantages:

i) Company deposits are not covered by DICGC like Bank deposits.
ii) The company fixed deposits are generally not emergency friendly as they may charge a higher penalty as compared to bank deposits in case of premature withdrawal.
iii) A company with a poor credit rating may offer a higher interest rate but investing in such a company can put your capital at risk.
iv) These deposits are unsecured and governed by the Companies Act. Therefore, the investor cannot sell the documents to recover his capital.

21.
FLOATING RATE SAVINGS BONDS (TAXABLE) – 2020

The government of India has launched Floating Rate Savings Bonds (Taxable) scheme with effect from July 01, 2020, generally known as GOI Bonds with an interest rate of 7.15% p.a. However, the interest rate on these bonds will be reset every six months every 1st July and 1st January and the coupon rate will be linked/pegged with prevailing National Saving Certificate (NSC) rate with a spread of (+) 35 bps over the respective NSC rate. In simple words, GOI bonds shall carry 0.35% interest extra over prevailing NSC interest rates, which at present are 6.80%.

The scheme is open for subscription from July 2020 through all nationalized banks and select private banks i.e. Axis Bank, ICICI Bank, HDFC Bank, and IDBI Bank.

These bonds are issued only in electronic form and held in the Bond Ledger Account (BLA). The BLA is an account with RBI or an agency bank in which the bonds are held. You will receive a certificate of holding from RBI/Agency Banks.

All resident Indians are eligible for investment in these bonds either individually or on a joint basis. These bonds can be taken on behalf of a minor also as a father/mother/legal guardian. Hindu Undivided Families are also allowed but Non-resident Indians (NRIs) are not allowed to invest in these bonds.

The Bonds shall be repayable on the expiration of 7 years from the date of issue and premature redemption shall be allowed for specified categories of Senior Citizens only with the penalty. The interest shall be payable semi-annually from the date of issue of bonds, up to 30th June/31st December as the case may be, and thereafter half-yearly for the period ending 30th June and 31st December on 1st July and 1st January respectively. There is no cumulative interest payment option for these bonds. The investors must provide bank account details to facilitate payment of interest/maturity proceeds directly to their bank account.

A minimum of Rs. 1,000/- can be invested in these bonds and in multiple of Rs.1,000/- with no maximum limit. As the name suggests, income from these bonds is taxable and tax will be deducted at source (TDS) while interest is paid. If you wish to seek an exemption under the relevant provisions of the IT Act, 1961, it has to be declared in the Application Form. These bonds are not tradable in the secondary market and are also not eligible as collateral for availing of loans.

Let's summarize the pros-n-cons of GOI Bonds:

a) **Advantages:**

   i) The main attractive feature of the Bonds is the higher interest rates than any other similar option like fixed deposit, NSC, KVP, etc.
   ii) The interest rate on the Bonds is based on the floating rate system which will ensure that the investors receive interest based on the prevailing interest rates in the market.
   iii) The bonds are risk-free as the scheme is launched by the Government of India.
   iv) You will receive a periodical and regular income from the Bonds giving you a choice to use the income either for savings or for consumption.

b) **Disadvantages:**

   i) These are taxable bonds and TDS shall be deducted at the time of payment of interest.
   ii) There is no option for cumulative interest. You may lose out on the compounding effect of the interest amount if you are not interested in regular income.
   iii) Restrictions on transferability, the lock-in period criteria, and the non-tradability of these bonds make this an illiquid investment.

22.
MUTUAL FUNDS

One of the popular investment options in India is investing in mutual funds. It offers investors a safe route to invest in equities (shares). A mutual fund is formed when an Asset Management Company (AMC) pools investments from various individuals and institutional investors with common investment objectives. Your funds are managed by experienced Fund Managers who professionally manage the pooled investment by strategically investing in stocks/securities to generate maximum returns for the investors. Fund Managers are skilled professionals with having an in-depth understanding of markets.

The investors also called unitholders, make money through regular dividends/interest and capital appreciation. You can however choose to re-invest the capital gains via a growth option or earn a steady income by way of a dividend option.

Mutual funds investment may look complicated for first-time investors as it can be confusing at times. Understanding how mutual funds work is the first step in your investment journey.

As a first-time investor in mutual funds, the first step is to define your financial goals, budget, and time horizon as already explained earlier in detail. With a clear objective in your mind, you will be able to decide how much money you can set aside towards investing in Mutual Funds and such a decision must be made based on your risk profile.

The next step is to choose the right fund type as it takes more than reading about different mutual fund types to decide on the right category. Experts generally recommend a balanced or debt fund for first-time investors as it comes with minimal risk while offering steady returns. As so many mutual fund schemes are available in each category, you need to analyze and compare each scheme for Fund Manager's credentials, expense ratio, portfolio components, and assets under management.

You may consider investing in more than one mutual fund to diversify your portfolio and earn risk-adjusted returns. A portfolio of funds will help you diversify across asset classes and investment styles. It will also even out risks when one mutual fund underperforms, as the other funds make up for the loss maintaining the value of your portfolio.

It is always advisable for first-time investors to start investing in mutual funds via Systematic Investment Plans (SIP) as lump sum investment can put you at the risk of catching a stock market peak. SIP allows you to spread your investments over time and invest across market levels. The benefit of rupee cost averaging that comes with SIP also helps you average out the cost of your investment and earn higher returns over the long term. You can start investing with only Rs. 500 in a mutual fund through SIP, which may not be possible with most other investment options.

You cannot invest in a mutual fund if you have not completed the Know Your Customer (KYC) process. KYC is a government regulation for most financial transactions in our country to identify the source of funds and to prevent money laundering. The become KYC-Compliant, you just need a PAN Card and valid address proof. Further, to invest in mutual funds, you must activate internet banking on your bank account. Mutual funds also allow investments to be made through Debit/Credit Cards and cheques, but doing it via net banking is a more straightforward, fast, and secure process to make investments.

As regards working of a Mutual Fund, it may be noted that any change in the value of investments made in capital market instruments (shares, debentures, etc.) is reflected in the Net Asset Value (NAV) of the scheme. The NAV represents the net value of an entity and is calculated as the total value of the entity's assets minus the total value of its liabilities. In the context of mutual funds, the NAV represents the per share/unit price of the fund on a specific date or time. As per Securities and Exchange Board of India (SEBI) guidelines, the NAV of a plan is determined by dividing the net assets of the scheme by the number of outstanding units on the valuation date. Most funds compute NAV on daily basis on closing market prices and these are available on their websites.

Classification of Mutual Fund Schemes:

Mutual fund schemes can be classified by different categories i.e. by structure, by nature, by investment objective, and others.

i) Open-Ended Funds:

Funds that can sell and purchase units at any point in time are classified as Open-Ended Funds. An open-ended fund is not required to keep selling new units to the investors at all times but is required to always repurchase when an investor wants to sell his units. NAV of such funds is calculated every day. The majority of the schemes offered by Asset Management Companies are open-ended schemes. Like all mutual fund schemes, these also have an initial offer period when the scheme is launched. However, once the initial offer closes, new investors can still purchase units on any working day at the prevailing NAV. Similarly, the fund house will repurchase the units from investors, any time at the NAV.

ii) Close Ended Funds:

Funds that can sell a fixed number of units only during the New Fund Offer (NFO) period are known as Closed-ended funds. The corpus of these funds remains unchanged. After the closure of the offer, buying and redemption of units by the investors directly from funds are not allowed. These funds are listed on stock exchanges where investors can buy/sell units from/to each other. The trading is generally done at a discount to the NAV of the scheme. The NAV of these schemes is computed weekly.

iii) Equity Funds:

These funds invest major corpus into equities. However, the structure of the fund may be different for every scheme depending upon the fund manager's outlook on different stocks. Since these funds are equity-linked, they rank high on the risk-return matrix; therefore they are beneficial for a longer time horizon. These funds can be further sub-divided into the following categories depending upon their investment objective:

- Large-Cap Funds
- Mid-Cap Funds
- Small-Cap Funds
- Diversified Equity Funds
- Sector Specific Funds
- Tax Savings Funds (ELSS)

iv) Debt Funds:

The primary objective of these funds is to invest in debt instruments issued by government authorities, private companies, banks, and financial institutions. Thus, by nature of their investment, these funds ensure low risk and are generally able to provide stable income to the investors. These funds can be further classified as under:

- Gilt Funds
- Income Funds
- Monthly Income Plans (MIP)
- Short Term Plans (STP)
- Liquid Funds

v) Balanced Funds:

As the name suggests, these funds invest in both equities and fixed income securities, which are in line with a pre-defined investment objective of the scheme and aim to provide investors with the best of both i.e. stability and growth.

Going by the investment objective, these funds can be further classified as:

1. Growth Schemes:

These schemes normally invest a major part of their fund in equities and are willing to bear a short-term decline in value for possible future appreciation. These schemes are also known as equity schemes and they aim to provide capital appreciation.

2. Income Schemes:

Also known as Debt Funds, they aim to provide regular and steady income to the investors. Therefore, these schemes generally invest in fixed income securities such as Bonds and Debentures, therefore may provide limited capital appreciation.

3. Balanced Schemes:

These schemes aim to provide both growth and income by periodically distributing a part of the income and capital gains earned. These schemes generally invest in equities and fixed income securities in the ratio of 50:50 or as indicated in their offer document.

4. Money Market Schemes:

These schemes aim to provide easy liquidity, capital protection, and moderate-income. Their investments are mainly in safer, short-term instruments e.g. Treasury Bills, Certificate of Deposits, Commercial Paper, and Inter-bank Call Money.

Other schemes can be categorized as Tax Saving Schemes where contribution made to any ELSS mutual fund is eligible for deduction under limits provided in Section 80C of the Income Tax Act. In Sector Specific Schemes, the investments are made by these funds in stocks of specific categories like FMCG, IT, Pharma, Petroleum, etc.

Exchange-Traded Funds (ETF)

Exchange-Traded Funds, commonly known as ETFs, are a collection of various securities such as bonds, shares, money market instruments, etc., that often track an underlying asset. ETFs are similar to mutual funds in terms of their structure, regulation, and management. Like 'Mutual Funds', they are a pooled investment vehicle that offers diversified investment into various asset classes like stocks, commodities, bonds, currencies, options, or a blend of these. Further, they can even be traded like stocks on the stock exchanges.

An ETF consists of shares that constitute widely followed indices such as NSE Nifty 50 and BSE SENSEX. If an ETF is tracking a particular index, then that index would contain the same stocks like that of the index, and their weightage shall also be the same. Additionally, the ETF may also invest in money market instruments for the sake of liquidity. ETF returns are generally predictable and will be close to what its underlying index earns. Even though many ETFs track the same index, their returns will not be the same as their debt holding differ, which affects their returns.

There are more than 100 ETFs in India as of the date and the following type of ETFs are available to suit the demands of almost all the investors:-

1. Bond ETFs:

Investing in Bond ETFs is a good way to mitigate the ups and downs of investing and diversifying a portfolio.

2. Currency ETFs:

These securities allow an investor to participate in currency market transactions without purchasing a specific currency.

3. Inverse ETFs:

Such funds are designed to return the opposite of what is offered by the underlying market index. With these funds, share prices move in the opposite direction of the inverse ETFs' share.

4. Liquid ETFs:

These funds endeavor to minimize price risks and enhance returns by investing in a basket of short-term government securities while simultaneously attempting to maintain liquidity.

5. Gold ETFs:

Such securities offer investors the opportunity to hold claims in the bullion market without any necessity to buy physical gold. There are other ETFs that focus on precious metals in general.

6. Index ETFs:

Index funds track the performance of their underlying index. They are further subdivided into replication and representative ETFs. Index funds that invest entirely in the securities underlying the index are called replication ETFs. On the other hand, representative ETFs are those that invest a majority of their fund corpus in representative samples and the remaining in other securities such as futures, options, etc.

Index Funds and exchange-traded funds might seem similar, but they are not the same. Although they are two of the most popular passive investment options if you are not sure as to which of the two suits you, then go through the following comparison:

PARAMETER	ETFs	Index Funds
Objective	Tracking the performance of indices of a particular exchange	Replicating the performance of a given index
How are they traded	Traded like a stock on an exchange	Units of index funds are issued like any other Mutual Fund
Pricing	The pricing follows the principles of shares	The NAV of the fund differs due to various factors
Factors affecting the price	Demand and Supply for the security in the market	NAV of the fund and the assets underlying.
Cost	A transactional fee is applicable	No transactional fee and commission
Expense Ratio	Low	High

As ETFs come at a lower cost, they carry a clear advantage over Index Funds but if you are not in a position to track the market and take timely decisions due to lack of knowledge or time constraints, you may invest in direct index funds as they are handled by professional managers and come at a lower cost than regular index funds.

As mentioned above, there are more than 100 ETFs in India to choose from. Funds like SBIETF IT, NIPPON INDIA ETF, NIPPON INDIA ETF NIFTY MIDCAP 150, NIFTY IT, ICICI PRUDENTIAL IT ETF, ICICI PRUDENTIAL MIDCAP 150 ETF, MOTILAL OSWAL MIDCAP 100 ETF are some of the currently better performing ETFs

How to Evaluate Mutual Funds:

Selecting the Mutual Fund Scheme which can meet your investment objective seems like a daunting task, but doing a little research and carrying out following due diligence before selecting a fund, will surely increase your chances of success.

i) Identify your Goals and Risk Tolerance:

Before investing in any fund, identify your goals for the investment, your risk tolerance capacity, time horizon i.e. how long to hold the mutual fund, and whether there are other alternatives to investing in mutual funds.

ii) Style and Fund Type:

Growth and capital appreciation funds generally do not pay any dividends as their primary objective is capital appreciation. If you are planning to invest for meeting your long-term need and can take the risk, these funds may be a good choice. If you need regular income from your portfolio, then investing in an income fund may be a better choice. Further, funds may also differentiate themselves by time horizons i.e. short, medium, and long term.

iii) Fees and Expenses:

Mutual Fund companies earn money by charging fees to the investor. It is, therefore, essential to understanding the different types of charges associated with an investment before making an investment decision. Some funds charge a sales fee known as a 'load'. It will either be charged at the time of purchase i.e. "front-end load" or upon the sale of the investment i.e. "back-end load". There is also a third type of fee, called a "Level-load fee" and it is an annual charge amount deducted from assets in the fund.

It is therefore advisable to look at the management expense ratio, which can help clear up any confusion relating to sales charges. The expense ratio is simply the total percentage of fund assets that are being charged to cover the fund expenses. The higher the ratio, the lower the investor's return will be at the end of the year.

iv) Passive Vs. Active Management:

The other important factor before investing in mutual funds is to consider your choice of "actively or passively" managed mutual funds.

In Actively managed funds, fund managers make decisions regarding which securities and assets to include in the fund based on their research. Generally, active funds seek to outperform a benchmark index, depending upon the type of the fund.

Passively managed funds, often called 'index funds', seek to track and duplicate the performance of a benchmark index. Passive funds do not trade their assets very often unless the composition of the benchmark index changes. This low turnover results in lower costs for the fund.

v) Evaluating Fund Manager's Performance and Past Results:

Before investing in a Mutual Fund, it is advisable to review the investment literature. The fund's prospectus should give you some idea of the prospects for the fund and its holdings in the years ahead. It is also important to research a fund's past results and performance of the fund manager, for example:

- Did the fund manager deliver results that were consistent with general market returns?
- Was the fund more volatile than the major indexes?
- Was there unusually high turnover that might impose costs and tax liabilities on investors?

vi) Size of the Fund:

Although the size of a fund does not hinder its ability to meet its investment objectives there are times when a fund can get too big. Although there is no set benchmark for how big is too big it makes it more difficult for a Fund Manager to efficiently run a fund if it is too big.

vii) History Often Doesn't Repeat:

We all are aware of the warning being given by the mutual funds themselves that "Past performance does not guarantee future results". The question here is why past results are so unreliable and why the experienced Fund Managers can replicate their performance year after year. Some actively managed funds beat the competition fairly regularly over a long period, but even the best minds in the business will have bad times. It's tempting to judge a mutual fund based on recent returns. However, if you want to pick a winner, look at how well it's poised for future success, not how it did in the past.

Let's summarize the pros-n-cons of investing in Mutual Funds:

a) **Advantages:**

i) It is relatively easier to buy and exit a mutual fund scheme. You can sell your open-ended equity mutual fund units when the stock market is high.
ii) Generally, Fund Managers spread investment across stocks of various companies in different sectors called 'diversification'. In this way, if one asset class doesn't perform, the other sectors can compensate to avoid a loss to investors.
iii) Mutual Funds are managed by Professional Fund Manager who does extensive research and possesses better investment management skills which ensure higher returns to the investor. Moreover, the Fund Manager also decides on how long to hold the securities.
iv) As compared to direct investment in the capital market, Mutual Funds cost lesser e.g. savings in brokerage costs, de-mat costs, depository costs, etc.
v) Mutual Funds provide an investment with various schemes having different investment objectives thus giving an option to investors to invest in a scheme that suits their financial goals and objectives.
vi) Updated information on the value of your investment in addition to the complete portfolio of investments, the proportion allocated to different assets, and the Fund's investment strategy, Mutual Fund investment are 'transparent'.
vii) Mutual Fund investments are flexible because of options such as Systematic Investment Plan (SIP), Systematic Withdrawal Plan (SWP), and Dividend investment plans.
viii) Mutual Fund investments are relatively safe as fund houses are strictly under the purview of statutory government bodies like SEBI. They also have an impartial grievance redressal platform that works in the interest of the investors.

b) **Disadvantages:**

i) Investors have no right to participate in the decision-making process. Some investors find it as a constraint in achieving their financial goals/objectives.
ii) Many investors find it difficult to select one option from the plethora of funds/schemes/plans available.
iii) Mutual Funds generally charge fees as 'Exit Load' which discourages investors from redeeming investment for some time.

Investing is the intersection of economics and psychology.
-Seth Klarman

23.
INVESTMENT IN EQUITY SHARES

We have discussed many investment avenues available to the investors but investing in shares also called equity or stock is one of the most common investments made by investors as it can offer comparatively higher returns if invested for longer time horizons.

Although Mutual Funds are the indirect route of investing in shares due to limitations to the investor in the decision-making process while selecting a particular stock/industry, etc., many investors wish to directly invest in shares to buy their preferred stocks. Moreover, investing in the stock market is the most common way for beginners to gain investment experience.

Let's first understand what it means by equity, typically referred to as shareholders' equity, it represents the amount of money that would be returned to a Company's shareholder if all of the assets were liquidated and all of the company's debt was paid off in the case of liquidation. Thus, a share is the smallest unit of ownership in a company i.e. if you own a share; you are a part-owner of that company.

Although investing in equities is a high-risk investment but various research and studies have proved that equities have outperformed most other investments in the long run. Equities have given around 17% returns to investors in terms of increase in share prices or capital appreciation annually from 1990 onwards till date. Therefore, equities are considered the most challenging but rewarding investment as compared to other investment options. Legendary investor Warren Buffett defines investing as "the process of laying out money now in the expectation of receiving more money in the future".

Investment In Equity Shares

Before buying a company's share, it is important to conduct thorough research on the company's background. Before investing you should consider the following factors:

a) The company's revenue model
b) The company's management stability
c) The company's competitors, etc.

Further, while investing in the stock market, it is important to maintain a diverse portfolio. You should mix up different sectors in your portfolio so that your portfolio is not uniquely vulnerable to the ups and downs in one sector. You should also look to invest in large-cap companies for stable but small returns, and small-cap companies for large but unreliable returns.

There are two ways of investing in the share market i.e. Primary & Secondary. The primary way of investing in the share market includes applying for shares when a company comes out with a public issue i.e. Initial Public Offer (IPO). You can also invest in the primary market through Follow-on Public Offer (FPO). FPO is issued by a company that already has shares trading in the secondary market. The other way of investing in the share market is through buying/selling the shares of already-listed companies on a stock exchange.

As many investors tend to invest in Initial Public Offers, it is always advisable to find answers to the following questions before making an investment decision:

- Who are the Promoters?
- Who is the Board of Directors?
- Is the price justified?
- What are the key risk factors?
- What are the products/services of the company?
- What is the size of the issue?
- What is the promoter's holding after the issue?
- How are the key financial ratios of the company e.g. Earnings per Share (EPS), Price Earning Ratio (P/E), Return on Capital (ROC), Debt/Equity ratio, Earnings, etc?

Terms like EPS, P/E, ROC EBITDA, Debt/Equity ratio, etc. are very commonly used in determining the potential of a share. Therefore, whether you are going to invest in the primary market or secondary market, you must have a fair idea of these terms and how they can help you in making an investment decision.

Earnings per Share (EPS):

EPS is calculated as the company's profit divided by the outstanding shares. The resulting number serves as an indicator of a company's profitability. The higher a company's EPS, the more profitable it is considered to be.

EPS = Net Income/average outstanding common shares

Price Earnings Ratio (P/E):

The Price-to-earnings ratio is a quick way to see if a stock is undervalued or overvalued. Generally, the lower the P/E ratio is, the better it is for the business and potential investors.

P/E = Current stock price/EPS

Return on Capital (ROC):

Return on capital (ROC), or return on invested capital (ROIC), or return on capital employed (ROCE), is a ratio used in finance, valuation, and accounting, as a measure of the profitability and value-creating potential of companies relative to the amount of capital invested by the shareholders and other debt-holders. In other words, this ratio can help to understand how well a company is generating profits from its capital as it is put to use. While there is no industry standard, a higher return on capital employed suggests a more efficient company, at least in terms of capital employed.

ROC = EBIT / Capital Employed

EBIT – Earnings before Interest and Taxes

Capital Employed – Total assets – current liabilities

Debt-Equity Ratio:

The debt-equity ratio is a measure of the relative contribution of the creditors and shareholders or owners in the capital employed in business i.e. ratio of the total long-term debt and equity capital is called the debt-equity ratio. A ratio greater than 1 implies that the majority of the assets are funded through debt whereas a ratio less than 1 implies that the assets are financed mainly through equity. Generally, a good debt-to-equity ratio is around 1 to 1.5 but it varies from industry to industry.

Debt-equity ratio = Total liabilities/Total shareholders' equity

The other critical profitability metrics for any company which every investor must understand include 'gross profit' and 'net income'. Gross profit also referred to as Gross Income represents the income or profit remaining after the production costs have been subtracted from the amount of income generated from the sale of a company's goods and/or services. The gross profit helps investors to determine how much profit a company earns from the production and sale of its goods and services.

On the other hand, net income is the profit that remains after all expenses and costs have been subtracted from revenue. Net profit also referred to as net income helps investors determine a company's overall profitability, which reflects on how effectively a company has been managed.

A share market is a place where buyers and sellers meet for the exchange of shares. To facilitate the exchange publicly, a formal marketplace has been developed for investors to buy and sell their shares. In India, people trade stocks on the following two platforms:

a) Bombay Stock Exchange (BSE) – Established in 1875, it is the oldest stock exchange in Asia.
b) National Stock Exchange (NSE) – This is the largest stock exchange in India.

However, to gain access to these exchanges, retail investors need to register with brokerage firms or Depository Participants (DP) first. It is important to find the right DP as you will buy, store, and sell stocks through them. They will provide the interface through which you will interact with the stock market.

It is advisable to open an electronic 2-in-1 Demat and Trading Account with a DP as these accounts let you trade in stocks from the convenience of your home. An electronic account is also helpful as it lets you see all your positions at a single glance. Certain DPs provide real-time market data to registered users and in the stock market, information is money. Therefore, choose your broker or DP thoughtfully before you start trading.

To open a Demat account to store your positions electronically and a trading account to execute the trades, the following documents are required:

i) PAN Card
ii) Adhaar Card
iii) Canceled cheque with your name printed on it
iv) Identity Proof
v) Residence Proof
vi) e-KYC – certain DPs will let you link your Adhaar Card to your trading account
vii) Additional information like annual salary range, etc.

The stock market is a lucrative means of investing and can generate high returns. However, it is a risky investment, therefore, as a beginner; invest in the stock market with money that you can afford to lose. Always remember, "Best judgment comes from experience and experience comes from bad judgment". Don't be afraid of ups and downs in the stock market, stay invested for a while, keep trading limits e.g. upside 20% and lower side minus 5% to start with, and keep enhancing your investment skills by talking to experienced people, browsing the internet, reading books, etc.

Let's summarize the pros-n-cons of investing in equity:

a) **Advantages:**

i) The biggest advantage of share market investment is that it has the potential to generate inflation-beating returns within a short period as compared to other investment options.
ii) The shares of the Company which is listed on stock exchanges have the benefit of any time liquidity. The shareholders can very easily transfer ownership.

Investment In Equity Shares

iii) The liability of a shareholder is limited to the extent of the investment made. If the company goes into losses, the share of loss over and above the capital investment would not be borne by the investor.

iv) By investing in the company, the shareholder gets ownership in the company and thereby he can exercise control i.e. he gets voting rights in the company.

v) Whenever companies require further capital for expansion etc., they tend to issue 'right shares' to existing shareholders at a price lower than the current market price of the equity share.

vi) At times, companies decide to issue bonus shares to their shareholders which are free shares given to existing shareholders.

vii) Your rights are well protected as the stock market is regulated by the SEBI.

viii) Return on investment in equities are taxed differently i.e. Long term capital gains, short-term capital gains, and even capital loss can be offset or carried forward.

b) Disadvantages:

i) Equity share investment is a risky investment as compared to any other investment option because there is no collateral security attached to it.

ii) The market price of any equity share has a wide variation. It is often said; you can't buy a share at its lowest price and also can't sell at its highest price. You have to always settle for intermediate prices.

iii) An equity investor is a small investor in the company, it is, therefore, hardly possible to impact the decision of the company using the voting rights.

iv) An equity shareholder has a residual claim over both the assets and the income as he comes last in the list of stakeholders.

v) If you are buying stocks on your own, you have to do a lot of research to pick a profitable stock, which is a very tedious and time-consuming job.

vi) To many investors, investing in equity shares is like an emotional roller coaster. Since stock prices fluctuate every minute, they tend to constantly look at the price fluctuations of stocks.

24.
INVESTMENT IN GOLD

Gold is considered an indicator of wealth and prosperity in this world. It is seen as a safe-harbor asset that protects purchasing power against inflation during challenging economic times since it tends to hold its value over the long term despite fluctuations. Gold can survive both financial and geopolitical uncertainties, which is perhaps why most countries believe in having huge gold reserves which can be used to combat any situation. In our country gold is considered auspicious and our celebrations are not complete without it. A common Indian starts investing in gold for his daughter's marriage from the day she is born.

The salient features of investment in Gold:

1) Gold is perhaps the only element that retains its value and protects against inflation, with its value rising with the cost of living, often reaching its highest value during periods of high inflation. The average price of 10 gram gold in India was Rs.89/- in 1947, Rs.1330/- in 1980, Rs.4,400/- in 2000, Rs.18,500/- in 2010, and Rs.48,650/- in the year 2020.
2) Gold investment is seen as a safety net against market volatility, as the value of gold is inversely proportional to the stock market.
3) Gold, being a natural resource is in limited supply that ensures that there will always be a demand for it, raising its value in the market, thereby making it an excellent investment option.
4) Gold is an extremely liquid asset, offering investors the chance to trade it during emergencies as its high demand ensures that it is easy to sell, commanding a good value even during the most testing times.

5) Gold is a tangible asset that cannot be reproduced with a machine-like currency, therefore, protecting investors against currency devaluation.
6) Due to its ability to retain its value even during the most testing times, gold is referred to as the 'crisis commodity.
7) Investing in gold today has become very simple as an individual can invest in Gold in the physical form i.e. bars, coins, and jewelry, or opt to invest it through ETF, E-Gold, Gold Funds, etc. This offers flexibility and ease of owning gold, without having to worry about its safety.
8) Gold is the easiest form of obtaining a loan against security. Today, there are several companies in our country providing loans against gold besides almost all banks, and that also on competitive interest rates.
9) The Gold Monetisation Scheme (GMS) allows you to deposit your idle gold with a Reserve Bank of India (RBI) designated bank and earn interest on the same. This works similarly to a bank fixed deposit.

Ways to Investment in Gold:

1) Buying in physical form:

It is the simplest way of investing in gold by buying it in physical form i.e. coins, bars, or jewelry. However, while buying physical gold, you have to be cautious about the purity of the gold, especially when buying jewelry. It is, therefore, advisable to go for 'Hallmark' jewelry. Hallmarking indicates the purity in carat and fineness for gold as '916' stands for 22-carat gold, '750' stands for 18-carat gold, etc. Also, ensure that the hallmark on your gold jewelry must have a Bureau of Indian Standard (BIS) mark which is represented by a triangle. You must also look for jewelers' marks and Assaying and Hallmarking center's identification mark or number. To convert Carat into the percentage, you need to divide the carat number by 24 and multiply the result by 100. E.g. to find out the gold percentage in your 22-carat jewelry, divide 22 by 24, the result is 0.9166, multiply it with 100, the result will be 91.66% - that's the purity of your gold.

Although there's no investment charge involved in the physical buying of gold, however, you have to bear the making charges for jewelry or coins. Further, you are to bear the risk of theft/burglary associated with carrying around or storing the physical gold.

2) Gold Exchange Traded Funds (ETF):

It is somewhat similar to making a direct investment in gold, but here the investor buys proportionate ownership in the collective vault instead of buying the physical gold. These schemes invest in standard gold bullion with 99.5% purity. You need to have a Demat account for investing in gold ETF. As the investment in gold involves asset management and brokerage charges, the returns are comparatively lesser than the actual increased value of the gold. These gold ETFs are not affected by the stock market fluctuations.

3) Gold Mutual Funds:

The investment is made not in gold but in the companies involved in mining the gold therefore change in the price of gold does not affect Gold Mutual Funds directly. Besides a charge involved in the management of the fund, there are entry and exit charges that make the overall returns smaller than the actual increased value of gold. Gold MFs are affected by stock market fluctuations.

4) Sovereign Gold Bonds:

Sovereign Gold Bonds were introduced by the Government of India in the year 2015. The objective behind launching this scheme was to offer an alternative option for investment in solid gold. Usually comes with a 5-year lock-in period. Sovereign Gold Bonds can be redeemed in cash later.

5) Digital Gold:

Recently, digital gold has gained a lot of popularity in the financial marketplace. Fintech platforms provide the option of buying and selling gold just like any other digital transaction. However, you must analyze the market carefully before investing in digital gold to avoid forgery.

I was going through the scheme of "Tanishq" Digital Gold where you can start your golden savings journey with as low as Rs.100. You can sell anytime, without going anywhere, and receive money directly in your account or you can convert digital gold to physical gold in the form of jewelry.

Let's summarize the pros-n-cons of investment in Gold:

a) **Advantages:**

  i) Keeping the gold in physical form always provides a person with a sense of financial security.
  ii) Gold's value is inversely influenced by inflation i.e. its price goes up when the currency's purchasing power goes down.
  iii) Gold being a very popular investment option, there are a lot of platforms where you can easily buy or sell gold. This makes it easy for you to convert your investment into cash i.e. highest liquidity.
  iv) Besides diversifying your portfolio, gold investment is an excellent hedge against risks associated with market price fluctuations.
  v) You can escape the formalities of paperwork, etc. that come with other modes of investment, and no Demat account is needed for buying physical gold.

b) **Disadvantages:**

  i) You are subjected to high risks if physically accumulated gold is stored in the house or similar locations in terms of theft/burglary.
  ii) Buying gold in the physical form calls for making charges and other taxes.
  iii) Investment in gold doesn't give any sort of yield, unlike other assets that pay dividends. You can only get your return on investment (ROI) when you sell it.
  iv) Since gold has already established itself as a high-value commodity, you'll need substantial capital to invest in the precious metal.

25.
INVESTMENT IN REAL ESTATE

Owning a home is the dream of everyone and fulfilling this dream can not only give you emotional satisfaction but monetary joy also. Keeping in view the fact that there is an acute shortage of land in cities across the country, even a small flat can offer you returns, either in the form of rental income or by selling it for profit. It is a fact that real estate prices tend to increase steadily over a period and time, thus ensuring lucrative returns but it requires substantial investment and maybe the largest investment made by you.

The first consideration to be made before investing in real estate is to figure out whether you wish to invest in a home/commercial property and wish to make money by renting out the property or you wish to make money through appreciation of the property's value. The real-estate investment comes with several risks and first-time investors should keep the following points in mind before making investment decisions in real estate:

i) Check your Budget:

As property investment is substantial, it is essential that you check your finances i.e. how much are your savings, how much loan will be required and what should be the tenure of the loan, etc., and make your budget. It is suggested that you should start the search for the property only after deciding your budget and strictly maintaining plus/minus percentage over your budget e.g. +/- 10%. Otherwise, you may get lured to a property that although is very good but beyond your budget and still may get trapped in the deal putting you in many

Investment In Real Estate

financial hardships at a later date. We shall discuss housing loans, EMI, etc. separately.

ii) Stay Patient:

Buying a property is a time-consuming affair, exhibiting patience can help you get a good deal although many real estate firms/brokers may lure you with false promises. Decisions taken in hurry may land you in trouble as you may end up paying more prices for the property or project that is inordinately delayed blocking your investment or you purchase one which doesn't live up to your expectations.

iii) Do your homework:

With several projects coming up, it can be confusing to choose the right property e.g. site location, the reputation of the builder, price of similar size flat/house in the vicinity, the amenities on offer, quality of construction, etc. need thorough research. Good homework can save you from many problems at a later date.

iv) Check the Papers:

Buying a property without clear titles can lead you to long-drawn court cases or litigations thus blocking your hard-earned money. All property papers should be thoroughly checked and for this job, you should take the assistance of legal experts.

v) Check the market rates:

Local administration publishes area-wise circle rates for land/property which may be used as guidance value to ascertain property rates in a particular area. Knowing the market rates will help you to track local trends and will also caution you in case someone is selling properties below the market rate as such properties could have litigations or other internal/external issues.

vi) Learn the art of Negotiations:

Negotiations are key to a successful deal in the Indian real estate system. It is a fact that sellers keep certain freebies like parking space, choice of garden/pool facing flat, additional furniture/furnishings, etc. for which they will first ask you to pay an additional amount unless you negotiate with them and settle the price including these items. Remaining calm and composed while interacting with property sellers can help you get additional benefits.

vii) Consider the risk factors:

Although real-estate investments are considered safer than many other investments, that doesn't mean they are risk-free. Property disputes and legal hurdles are common in our country. Therefore, it is necessary to ensure that the property is free from all encumbrances. It is advisable to get yourself acquainted with RERA Act, The Benami Property Act, and the GST Act also.

Arranging Finances & availing Housing Loan:

Banks and other financial institutions generally offer housing loans up to 85% of loans against the value of a property. Besides, the value of property there are other expenses like stamp duty, registration, and other charges that banks normally don't cover which comes to about 10% of the value of the property. In simple terms, if you are looking for a property worth Rs. 1 crore, you should have Rs. 25 lacs in your hands as you may get a loan up to Rs.85 lacs for the said property.

Bank assess your repayment capacity while deciding the home loan eligibility which is based on your monthly disposable/surplus income i.e. monthly income less monthly expenses and other factors like spouse's income, assets, liabilities, stability of income, etc. Banks also look out for your age, educational background, industry in which you are employed, other loans availed, etc. Further, the amount of the loan depends on the tenure of the loan and the rate of interest as these variables determine your monthly outflow which in turn depends on your disposable income. Generally, you may get around 60 times of your net salary or monthly income as a home loan. There are following two types of housing loans that are offered:

1) Fixed Interest Rate Home Loan:

In this type of home loan, the interest rate remains fixed for the entire tenure of the loan irrespective of prevailing market interest rates. The fixed interest rate is higher than the floating interest rate.

2) Floating Interest Rate Home Loan:

In this type of home loan, the interest rate keeps fluctuating according to prevailing interest rates in the market according to the economic trends. In such loans, the EMI of the loan would increase or decrease depending on the interest rate movement. However, banks generally provide an option to increase the tenure of the loan, at a constant EMI, for borrowers who do not desire to pay increased EMIs in case of an increase in interest rates.

Re-payment of Home Loan:

You repay the loan in Equated Monthly Instalments (EMI) comprising both principal and interest. EMI generally starts from the month following the month in which you take full disbursement.

Let's assume you wish to avail a home loan of Rs. 50 lakh and the prevailing interest rate is 7% p.a. your EMI for different tenures will be as under:-

TENURE	EMI (Rs.)/per month	TOTAL INTEREST PAYABLE (Rs.)
10 years	58,054/-	19,66,509
15 years	44,941/-	30,89,454
20 years	38,765/-	43,03,587
25 years	35,339/-	56,01,688
30 years	33,265/-	69,75,445

However, if the rate of interest goes up by only 1% i.e. you avail of a home loan of Rs. 50 lakh @ 8% p.a. the calculations will be as under:-

TENURE	EMI (Rs.)/per month	TOTAL INTEREST PAYABLE (Rs.)
10 years	60,664/-	22,79,656
15 years	47,783/-	36,00,869
20 years	41,822/-	50,37,281
25 years	38,591/-	65,77,243
30 years	36,668/-	82,07,762

It is, therefore, necessary to keep in mind that although loans for longer durations are now easily available they cost you dearly as you end up paying huge interest. Further, you must look for better interest rates from different banks/financial institutions as even the difference of one percent in interest rate makes a huge difference e.g. for 30 years tenure, you pay Rs.12,32,317/- extra on Rs. 50 lakh loan. Try to negotiate with banks/financial institutions on interest rates, as there is always a scope of getting a good deal based on your CIBIL score, etc. which has been explained later in the book.

Although the above calculations may be seen favoring the short tenure of the loan it may also be kept in mind that due to inflation, the value of money shall keep decreasing and your income/salaries, perks, bonus, etc. may keep increasing. Therefore, to avoid the immediate burden of huge EMI, you may consider a loan for a longer duration and if any surplus amount is available with you, try to pre-pay the loan.

Tax Deductions on Home Loan:

A home loan must be taken for the purchase of a house/flat or construction of a house but the construction must be completed within five years from the end of the financial year in which the loan was taken.

In the case of payment of EMI, it has two components i.e. Principal repayment and Interest. The interest portion of the EMI paid for the year can be claimed as a deduction from your total income up to a maximum of Rs.2 lakh for 'self-occupied house' property whereas there is no upper limit for 'let out property' for claiming interest.

The principal repayment portion of the EMI paid for the year is allowed as a deduction under Section 80C with a maximum limit of Rs.1.50 lakh. It may please be noted that to avail of this deduction, the house property should not be sold within five years of possession, otherwise, the deduction claimed earlier will be added back to your income in the year of sale.

We have already discussed earlier that please ensure insurance of your house property against fire, theft, earthquake, etc. Moreover, it is always advisable to take Home Loan Insurance also which will cover the EMIs in case you meet with an accident, job loss, or similar fate which leaves you unable to make the payments.

Owning a house/flat is a great idea as discussed but you should avoid investing in the house property from your retirement proceeds as it will take away your significant retirement corpus and may land you in financial constraints at a later date. Although it is always better to enjoy the second innings of your life in your own house and if you have one, there is nothing better than it. However, even if you don't have a house/flat till retirement, please weigh all other options of investment and then only finalize investing in house property. Just, for example, a good 2 BHK flat in metro shall cost you around Rs.80 lakh and if you invest this 80 Lakh in other investment options even @ 7% interest p.a., you shall be getting Rs.5,60,000/- as interest whereas the same flat may be available on rent of Rs. 30,000/- per month, thus leaving Rs.2 lakh in your hand every year besides saving you from expenses on property taxes, maintenance, etc.

Let's summarize the pros-n- cons of Real Estate Investment:

a) Advantages:

i) Real estate investment gives you a sense of security and you can enjoy your investment by either using it for your purposes or leasing it out. Further, as real estate price does not fluctuate now and then as compared to the stock market, it won't keep you bothered with often checks.

ii) Real estate investment can generate steady cash flows for you, as you can either invest in a residential property or a commercial property and rent it out.

iii) Home Loan allows multiple tax benefits which significantly help you to reduce your tax outgo.

iv) Real estate is a straightforward and secure investment and gives you complete authority about each and everything involved in the venture.

v) Real estate values tend to increase over time resulting in profits when you sell them. Therefore, it is seen as hedging against inflation.

b) **Disadvantages:**

 i) Real estate investment is a lengthy procedure and requires a lot of documentation in compliance with statutory regulations, therefore need the advice of legal advisors to complete the entire buying process.
 ii) Background checks and price evaluation, etc. also involve a time commitment to figure out a perfect deal for the investment.
 iii) Even if you rent out a property, you are liable as an owner to pay the maintenance cost of the property and property taxes.
 iv) There are high entry and exit costs involved in the real estate investment e.g. registration charges and stamp duty, etc.
 v) Real estate investments are not liquid investments as selling property also is a time-consuming process.
 vi) In the case of investment in commercial property by availing loan, there are no tax benefits on the EMIs being paid for the commercial property.

26.
CIBIL SCORE

We have discussed investment in Real Estate which is a significant investment and generally requires financing i.e. loan. In the next chapter, we shall discuss 'loan against securities'. Now a day, when you apply for any kind of loan, banks seek your credit history from CIBIL, and based on the CIBIL score, banks decide whether you are eligible for a loan or not. Moreover, good credit ratings can help you in negotiating better interest rates also.

TransUnion CIBIL Limited is India's first credit information company. They collect credit-related information from banks and financial institutions detailing loans and credit card payment history. Around 500 banks and financial institutions are clients of CIBIL. They report information relating to customers' actions which includes buying of a credit card, payment of credit card, payment of loan EMIs, the default of loan payment and even inquiry for a loan, etc. This report is generally known as Credit Information Report.

Based on the above credit information report, a 'credit score' of an individual customer is generated, which is used by the lenders during the loan evaluation process.

A CIBIL Credit Score is a 3 digit numerical score based on a statistical analysis of a person's credit history which represents his creditworthiness. The value ranges from 300 – to 900. Loan eligibility is determined using information such as Income, Current EMIs, and Credit Score. In more than 90% of cases, loans are granted to only those individuals whose credit score is above 750.

Let's look at 'CIBIL Score' and what does it mean:

CIBIL SCORE 850-900

It indicates that you have never defaulted even once, thus it is an excellent score.

CIBIL SCORE 750-850

Although around 75-80% of loans are sanctioned for a credit score above 750, you can negotiate better terms and interest rates if your credit score is above 800 as it is considered high.

CIBIL SCORE 700-750

This score is considered good for 'secured loans' only. However, in the case of unsecured loans, lenders may investigate further and such loans may be offered at higher interest rates.

CIBIL SCORE 500-700

This score indicates that you have delayed or defaulted a few times in the past. With this score, your chances of getting Personal Loans are negligible.

CIBIL SCORE 300-500

For an individual with a credit score between 300-500, it will be impossible to get a loan from any bank or financial institution in the country as it indicates too many discrepancies in past loan repayments.

Factors that affect your CIBIL Score:

The CIBIL score is made up of following five main factors:

Payment history	:	35%
Credit Exposure	:	30%
Credit History	:	15%
Credit Types	:	10%
New Credit	:	10%

Major factors adversely affecting your CIBIL Score:

i) Irresponsible Payment Behaviour:

As indicated above, payment history comprises 35% weightage in the score. It is, therefore, important to pay your credit card bills and loan EMIs on time every month. Even 30-day delinquency can reduce your score by 100 points.

ii) High Credit Utilisation Ratio:

According to experts, you should ideally not exceed using 30% of your credit limit. If you are using over 50% of your credit limit, it can harm your score as having a high credit exposure indicates that you are at a higher risk of default.

iii) Outstanding Debts:

In case you have unpaid dues reflected in your credit report, it takes a toll on your score. It is advisable to pay off the outstanding dues on time even if the amount is small.

iv) Paying only the Minimum Amount Due:

If you constantly pay only the minimum amount due, it leads to the interest compounding on your outstanding balance and indicates that you may fall into a debt trap. Further, it also reflects poor repayment behavior, thus adversely affecting your credit score.

v) Not having a credit mix of 'secured' & 'unsecured loans':

Home loans and Auto Loan are considered secured loans while credit card is examples of unsecured loans. If you have a high number of only one type of credit, it can affect your score.

vi) Closing Old Credit Card Accounts:

Credit cards are a great tool to build credit history. Therefore, if you have used a particular credit card for a substantial number of years, it is advisable to keep it open as long as possible. If required, you may consider closing a relatively new card.

vii) Credit History:

If you have a long credit history, it helps lenders take a sound decision at the time of offering you credit. It is, therefore, advisable to focus on building a credit history in the earlier stage of life i.e. using a credit card and making timely payments, etc., so that when you apply for a home loan or car loan, you will have a good CIBIL Score.

Benefits of having a good CIBIL score:

- ❖ Quick approval for loans and credit cards without any hassles
- ❖ Comparatively cheaper interest rates on loans
- ❖ Better deals on Credit Cards with the higher credit limit
- ❖ Discount on processing fee and other charges for loan applications

CIBIL Report:

To decide whether to approve or reject your loan, banks generally look for the following things in your CIBIL Report:

- ❖ Existing loans and their dues, if any
- ❖ Existing Credit Cards and their dues, if any
- ❖ EMI or Credit card payment track record, even delay of few days in making such payment is reflected in the report
- ❖ Number of times you have applied for loans or credit cards in the past 5 years
- ❖ Your loan repayment potential
- ❖ Details of all bank accounts
- ❖ Number of times the address has been changed
- ❖ Spouse credit history and repayment record
- ❖ Any settlements occurred due to late payments/disputes.

Check your CIBIL Score:

It is very easy to obtain your latest CIBIL score directly from the official website of TransUnion CIBIL at https://www.cibil.com/freecibilscore. Every individual is allowed to check their CIBIL score for free once a year. If you have already used this opportunity, then you need to have the paid plan with a monthly, half-yearly, or yearly subscription. In case you observe any discrepancies in your CIBIL report, you should communicate with your banks to get the errors rectified immediately and they must inform the rectifications to CIBIL immediatley as CIBIL directly don't entertain any such complaint.

27.
LOAN AGAINST SECURITIES

'Loan' as such is considered a bad word especially when we are talking of wealth creation. However, at times, the loan comes as a savior to help us out in the hour of need, be it a medical emergency or any other exigency that we have not planned and the funds required are more than our savings. In such a situation, taking a loan is a better option and it can prove to be a blessing. It is also important to know that a loan carries an interest cost and we have to be aware of the options available so that we can pick a loan that not only meets our requirements but is less costly also.

There are two types of loans i.e. 'Secured Loans' and 'Unsecured Loans'. For availing secured loan, the borrower has to pledge some assets as collateral for the loan. The rate of interest for a secured loan is less than the unsecured loan. Whereas unsecured loans are offered without any security and as the lender carries extra risk, they charge a higher rate of interest. Credit Cards and Personal Loans are examples of unsecured loans.

Secured loan i.e. loan against securities can be availed by pledging any of the following assets in your possession:

1) Loan against Gold:

A loan against gold is the best possible secured loan option for availing of a quick loan and at a lower rate of interest. You can pledge gold jewelry lying in your locker to take a loan from Banks or many other companies providing gold loans and mitigate your immediate financial needs. These loans are processed very fast, without any pre-processing charges, and with very little documentation.

2) Loan against Insurance Policies:

In case of need, availing loan against the LIC Endowment policy is the best option, if you have one as LIC gives up to 90% of the surrender value of the policy at comparatively lower interest rates than charged by banks. Although banks also offer loans against LIC policy, they give generally up to 80% of the surrender value and the loan offered by banks is on prevailing interest rates.

Borrowers can get a loan against Life Insurance Policies issued by LIC and other private insurance companies provided they are permanent and whole life policies and are not the term insurance policies as term insurance policies do not have any cash value.

3) Loan against Fixed Deposits:

If your cash requirement is for the short or medium-term and you have a fixed deposit, it is advisable to avail loan against pledging the same with the bank instead of breaking the FD in times of emergency as on making the FD again, you will be losing the power of compounding on your existing FD. You may get up to 80% of the FD amount as a loan at an interest rate that will be around 2% higher than the interest that you are getting on your FD.

Further, nowadays interest rates are reducing day by day and if you break the FD to meet exigency and later if you wish to again invest in Fixed Deposit, you may end up getting lower interest rates.

4) Loan against NSC/KVP:

You can also get a loan against the Post Office National Savings Certificate (NSC) or Kisan Vikas Patra (KVP) from banks that offer loans up to 80-85% of the value at the prevailing rate of interest. However, availing loan against NSC/KVP is a time-consuming process as you have to make an application to the post office to pledge your NSC/KVP in favor of the bank from where you wish to avail loan and such application has to be signed by the lender and borrower both. Only on receipt of the NSC/KVP duly marked as pledged, the bank will disburse the loan.

5) Loan against Shares and Mutual Funds:

You can take a loan against your shares and mutual funds also but as these instruments are highly volatile, banks generally give up to 50% of the current value of the shares/mutual funds. Further, each bank has its approved list of shares and mutual funds schemes and its own rules for giving loans against these types of securities.

6) Loan against Public Provident Fund (PPF):

If you are having a PPF account, you can avail loan up to 25% of the balance in the account 2 years back in its 3rd to 6th year.

7) Loan against Property:

If you require a loan for a bigger amount i.e. more than Rs. 10 lacs then you can consider availing loan against your residential or commercial property. Banks generally give up to 50% of the market value of the property or up to 40% of your monthly income. However, processing such a loan is a time-consuming process, and a lot of documentation is required for availing loan against property. You may also be required to pay processing charges for such a loan and interest rates are also on the higher side.

There are many other securities against which also you can take a secured loan but each bank has its own rule in this regard e.g. NABARD Bonds, Non-Convertible Debentures, RBI Bonds, Gold ETF, etc.

28.
REVERSE MORTGAGE

The life expectancy in India has risen steadily due to enhanced medical facilities in the last few decades and most of the families are now nuclear families i.e. husband, wife, and children. Gone are the days when we Indians were enjoying the benefits of the joint family ensuring the safety and security of our financial and other needs in the second innings of our life. Senior Citizens, who don't have a regular income or who either don't have financial support from their children or they do not want to be dependent on them for their regular household expenses, medical expenses and other exigencies are finding it difficult to sustain their financial independence. The Reverse Mortgage introduced by the Government of India in 2007 has allowed senior citizens to spend their retired life peacefully and with dignity.

In simple terms, a reverse mortgage is the 'opposite' of a conventional home loan where we are required to pay regular Equated Monthly Instalments (EMI) for the chosen period of the loan. A reverse mortgage enables a senior citizen to receive a regular stream of income from a bank or a financial institution against the mortgage of his home. However, the borrower and his/her spouse continue to reside in the property till the end of their life and receive a periodic payment on it.

When the home is pledged, its monetary value is arrived at by the bank, based on the demand for the property, its current valuation, and the condition o the house. The bank after considering a margin for interest costs and price fluctuations disburses a loan amount to the borrower in the form of periodic payments also known as "Reverse EMI" over the fixed loan tenure.

The Reserve Bank of India has formulated the following guidelines for a reverse mortgage:-

- The maximum loan amount would be up to 60% of the value of the residential property. However, many banks which offer Reverse mortgages have capped the maximum loan up to Rs. 1 Crore.
- The minimum tenure of the mortgage is 10 years and the maximum is 15 years. However, some banks are now offering a maximum tenure of 20 years.
- Banks offer the option of monthly, quarterly, annual, or lump-sum loan payments.
- Property revaluation is to be undertaken by the lender (bank) once every 5 years. If at such time, the valuation has increased, borrowers have the option of increasing the quantum of the loan.
- Amount received through a reverse mortgage is a loan and not income. Therefore, it will not attract any tax.
- Reverse mortgage interest rates could be either fixed or floating. The rate would be determined based on the prevailing market interest rates.

Eligibility Criteria:

- A reverse mortgage is available to house owners above the age of 60 years. However, in case a couple wishes to opt, the age of the spouse should be more than 58 years.
- The borrower must have a self-acquired, self-occupied residential house or flat, located in India. The titles should be clear, indicating the prospective borrower's ownership of the property. In the case of a couple, at least one of them must own a house.
- The Property should be free from any encumbrances.
- The property must have been in existence for at least 20 years.
- Property should be the permanent primary residence of the individuals i.e. properties that are let out or used for commercial purposes are not eligible for a reverse mortgage.

Salient Features of Reverse Mortgage:

i) A borrower can pre-pay the loan at any point during the term of the loan without attracting a pre-payment penalty or charges.

ii) If the borrower outlives the tenure of the loan, he could continue to stay in the house. However, a bank may cease the monthly payments. Settlement of the loan is done only after the borrower's death.

iii) If one of the spouses dies, the other can continue living in the house. Only on the death of both, settlement of the loan takes place.

iv) The loan could be foreclosed by the bank only if:
   a) The borrower has not stayed in the house for a continuous period of one year.
   b) The borrower has not paid property taxes and fails to insure the home.
   c) If the borrower makes changes in the residential property, that could affect the security of the loan. This could be renting out part or an entire house, the addition of a new owner to the house's title, or creating further encumbrance on the property.
   d) If the government under statutory provisions seeks to acquire or condemn the residential property for health or safety reasons.
   e) If the mortgaged property is donated or abandoned by the borrower.
   f) If the borrower declares himself as bankrupt.

v) A reverse mortgage loan becomes due when the last surviving borrower dies, or if the borrower chooses to sell the house. The bank first gives an option to the next of kin to settle the loan along with accumulated interest, without the sale of a property. If the next of kin are unable to settle the loan, the bank then opts to recover the same from the sale proceeds of the property.

vi) Any extra amount, after settlement of the loan with accrued interest and expenses, through the sale of the property, will be passed on to the legal heirs.

vii) If the sale proceeds are lower than the accrued interest plus the principal amount, the loss is borne by the bank.

Types of Reverse Mortgage in India:

1. Normal Reverse Mortgage:

Under the normal reverse mortgage loan, the residential property of the borrower is pledged to the lender and the lender directly pays out either a lump-sum amount or makes period payments directly to the house owner, who also happens to be the borrower, without intermediaries.

2. Reverse Mortgage Loan Enabled Annuity (RMLEA)

Reverse mortgage loan enabled annuity is an extension of the reverse mortgage. Under RMLEA, the bank pays a one-time lump sum to a life insurer of the borrower's choice, to avail immediate annuity plan. The chosen life insurer then makes monthly payments across the lifetime of the borrowers. This regular payment is called 'annuity'.

The money received by the annuity is more than what a normal reverse mortgage borrower receives as a life insurer gets a lump-sum payment.

Though introduced in 2007, Reverse Mortgage has not gained much popularity in India as many of the senior citizens are not aware of this product due to its inadequate marketing. Further, many senior citizens see their home as their legacy which they want to leave behind, or in some cases, children have resentment for a reverse mortgage as they see it as giving away their family property. However, as a financial tool, Reverse Mortgage is ideal to augment a senior citizen's income in the years ahead and make good the shortfall in one's pension or income to live a quality retired life.

Let's summarize the pros-n-cons of Reverse Mortgage:

a) Advantages:

i) A reverse mortgage allows a senior citizen to turn an otherwise illiquid asset into cash which can be used to meet regular expenses.

ii) A reverse mortgage allows you to live in your home to which your emotions are attached and without fear of losing your neighborhood or downsizing your home in case of a sell-off.

- iii) You can use the proceeds of a reverse mortgage to pay off an existing home loan. This will give you more amounts in your hands.
- iv) The income you receive from the bank will be tax-free. Moreover, if the house is renewed or repaired with this money, the amount spent on the renewal or repairs will be eligible for deduction in the computation of income.
- v) In some cases, the value of your home could end up being less than the total amount owed on the reverse mortgage. Even if this occurs, your heirs don't have to worry about paying the balance.
- vi) An availing reverse mortgage with an annuity offers higher income.

b) **Disadvantages:**

- i) There are a lot of rules and caveats to reverse mortgage loans. You should be wary of any reverse mortgage offer unless you understand the terms well.
- ii) Availing Reverse Mortgage may require a lengthy and cumbersome documentation process.
- iii) Lenders usually charge 2-3% higher interest rates, when compared to a simple mortgage.
- iv) Since staying current on property taxes, insurance, maintenance, etc. is mandatory to avail of the reverse mortgage, you must have plenty of cash flow for these expenses.
- v) It is a traditional practice in our country to transfer debt-free assets to the next generation. Therefore, owing to societal pressure, many senior citizens don't opt for a reverse mortgage, even though there is a need for it.
- vi) As a reverse mortgage does not require monthly payments, the interest is not deducted each month. This results in the amount accumulating over time and growing larger.
- vii) If you avail reverse mortgage loan, you and your spouse have to reside on this property and it cannot be rented out even partially.

29.
RETIREMENT PLANNING

While 'death' is considered the most uncertain thing in one's life but 'retirement' is one of the most certain things and it is also a fact that we can't keep working till we are alive. The time will come when we have to hang our boots and say goodbye to our working life. In India, the retirement age for service personnel is fixed at 60 years in Government, public sector, and many other companies. Even if you are self-employed, you can't continue working after a certain age. Thus, it is important to plan for your retired life as early as possible. However, the fact is that we do not pay much attention to our 'retirement plan', especially at a younger age. It is only when retirement comes nearer, we start worrying about our retired life and how to meet our financial needs.

Many studies have proved that over 70% of adults worry about money that takes a toll on their physical health. Financial stress is also linked to physical conditions such as Diabetes, Heart Disease, migraines, Headaches, and the most common is poor sleep. As the financial needs are related to sustenance issues, they may also cause anxiety and depression, thus, robbing you of peace of mind to enjoy your life today.

With the advancement of medical facilities, individuals are now living longer and as such, they will have more years to live after retirement i.e. they will require more money to sustain retired life. Therefore, while doing your retirement planning, please remember that:

1. Sufficient money is available upon retirement for monthly household expenses, medical expenses, and exigencies /emergencies.

2. To meet the needs of dependent family members for higher education, marriages, and other liabilities.
3. To support the fulfillment of your dreams, wishes, and aspirations such as dream vacations or maintaining your current lifestyle without any compromises.
4. Sufficient money must be available to ensure financial independence till you are alive.
5. Not only you will longer be due to changes in lifestyle and advanced medical care thus requiring more money, but you will also require more funds to beat inflation.
6. You may not have the zeal to work for long or after a certain age to meet your financial requirements and therefore retirement planning needs to be done at an early stage.

Retirement planning should include determining time horizons, estimating expenses, calculating required after-tax returns, assessing 'risk-tolerance', and doing estate planning. Start planning for retirement as soon as you can to take advantage of the 'power of compounding. Retirement plans evolve through the years which means portfolios should be rebalanced and financial plans updated as and when needed.

Steps to Retirement Planning:

1. The first step in retirement planning is to ascertain when you wish to retire and how long you have before retirement i.e. 10, 20, or 30 years.
2. You need to ascertain how much money you can spare for investing in retirement schemes after meeting your monthly expenses and keeping some money handy for emergencies.
3. Calculate your average expenses during retired life i.e. groceries, utilities, insurance, medical expenses, tax liabilities, etc. keeping into account the inflation.
4. Think of ways to convert savings into monthly income. It is a fact that retirees who receive regular monthly pension or annuity maintain a happier lifestyle in comparison to those who did not have a pension or annuity. Regular monthly income from your investments will give you a sense of confidence to meet your monthly expenses with ease.

5. Learn about your healthcare options and how much money will be required to take care of your medical needs so also your dependents as old age comes with many health issues.
6. Your retirement planning must include your dream vacations, fulfillment of your wishes, etc.
7. Knowing retirement could last 20, 30 years, or maybe more, the best time to start planning is today. Begin thinking about the ways and means to maximize your savings and supplement retirement options with your present monthly income.

One of the most challenging aspects of creating a comprehensive retirement plan is striking a balance between realistic return expectations and a desired standard of living. It is, therefore, always advisable to focus on creating a flexible portfolio that can be modified/updated regularly vis-à-vis changing market conditions and your retirement objectives.

The burden of retirement planning is falling on individuals now more than ever as we have also adopted the nuclear family system. We, therefore, can't depend upon our children also for our second innings. Early retirement planning is necessary for a sustainable financial goal. With an updated financial plan in place, you get to accomplish all your financial objectives.

The most significant thing in retirement planning is to reach a correct retirement corpus amount keeping in mind the 'inflation' e.g. a liter of milk used to cost Rs. 25/- in the year 2010 but now one liter of the same milk costs Rs. 50/- in 2022. Although we generally say milk has become costlier but the fact is the value of your rupee has gone down by approximately 50% during the period. Therefore, the same amount of Rs. 25/- will now get you only half a liter of milk. To make it more clear, assuming your monthly expenses today are Rs.20,000/- and you are planning to retire after 30 years. To maintain the same standard of living, you will require around Rs.1,20,000/- per month assuming inflation @ 6% p.a. and around Rs.4,00,00/- when you will be reaching 80 years of age. If we quantify the retirement amount required to sustain the same standard of living, it will be a big figure i.e. approximately Rs.5 crores considering the present interest rate scenario but it is misleading as during your retired life also, your investments should be such which keep yielding the returns to beat the inflation.

This has been explained through various examples and spreadsheets in the chapter relating to retirement planning for senior citizens. However, at a younger age, your retirement planning should preferably start as under:-

1. Employees' Provident Fund (EPF)

My first choice is EPF as in EPF, the employee and employer both contribute 12% or more of the pay of the employee. Further, in many organizations, there is a system of a voluntary contributions to PF, where employees can contribute more while there is no such obligation on the employer. It is mandatory for all the firms that employ 20 or more people to offer this benefit to employees. The interest rates are decided by the Central Board of Trustees of the fund every year which currently is 8.5% p.a. i.e. one of the highest interest rates on investment as of date. The money can be withdrawn on retirement or while leaving the firm. In the second case, there is an option to transfer the accumulated PF in the account opened with a new employer.

2. Public Provident Fund (PPF):

My second choice is Public Provident Fund (PPF). The detailed scheme has already been explained above. If you have any amount between Rs.1000/- to Rs.10,000/- every month to spare from your net take-home pay, open the PPF Account immediately and start depositing the same in the PPF Account. The biggest advantage of the PPF Account is that it can be maintained after retirement also and that will help you in beating inflation even during your retired life. Currently, a maximum of Rs.1,50,000/- per annum can be deposited in PPF Account in a maximum of 12 installments.

Let's understand the 'power of compounding with the tables given below:

TABLE 1:

Assuming you start depositing Rs.1,20,000/- every year in PPF Account at the age of 30 and continue it till you turn 60 years.

Retirement Planning

From 61st year onward, you start withdrawing Rs.12,20,000/- p.a. and keep depositing Rs. 1,20,000/- till the age of 80 years. You will still be left with Rs.44,00,000/- approximately when you turn 81. The biggest advantage is that it gives you confidence that you always have money at your disposal after the 7th year onward to meet any exigency/emergency.

It means you will have Rs.11,00,000/- every year for your monthly expenses and if your spouse is also working and he/she also starts saving only Rs.10,000/- per month, then you will have Rs.22,00,000/- every year to enjoy your second innings.

PPF DEPOSIT @ RS.10000/- PM (Rs.1,20,000/- every year from the age of 30)						
Op. Bal.	Intt. Rate	Cl.bal.	Interest	Withdrawal	Annual Dep.	Year
0	0.071	0	0	0	120000	Apr-22
120000	0.071	128520	8520	0	120000	Apr-23
248520	0.071	266165	17645	0	120000	Apr-24
386165	0.071	413583	27418	0	120000	Apr-25
533583	0.071	571467	37884	0	120000	Apr-26
691467	0.071	740561	49094	0	120000	Apr-27
860561	0.071	921661	61100	0	120000	Apr-28
1041661	0.071	1115619	73958	0	120000	Apr-29
1235619	0.071	1323347	87729	0	120000	Apr-30
1443347	0.071	1545825	102478	0	120000	Apr-31
1665825	0.071	1784098	118273	0	120000	Apr-32
1904098	0.071	2039289	135191	0	120000	Apr-33
2159289	0.071	2312599	153309	0	120000	Apr-34
2432599	0.071	2605313	172714	0	120000	Apr-35
2725313	0.071	2918810	193497	0	120000	Apr-36
3038810	0.071	3254565	215755	0	120000	Apr-37
3374565	0.071	3614159	239594	0	120000	Apr-38
3734159	0.071	3999284	265125	0	120000	Apr-39
4119284	0.071	4411753	292469	0	120000	Apr-40
4531753	0.071	4853507	321754	0	120000	Apr-41
4973507	0.071	5326625	353119	0	120000	Apr-42
5446625	0.071	5833335	386710	0	120000	Apr-43

5953335	0.071	6376022	422686	0		120000	Apr-44
6496022	0.071	6957239	461217	0		120000	Apr-45
7077239	0.071	7579722	502483	0		120000	Apr-46
7699722	0.071	8246402	546680	0		120000	Apr-47
8366402	0.071	8960416	594014	0		120000	Apr-48
9080416	0.071	9725124	644709	0		120000	Apr-49
9845124	0.071	10544127	699003	0		120000	Apr-50
10664127	0.071	11421279	757152	0		120000	Apr-51
11541279	0.071	12360709	819430	0		120000	Apr-52
12480709	0.071	13366839	886129	1220000		120000	Apr-53
12266839	0.071	13137783	870945	1220000		120000	Apr-54
12037783	0.071	12892465	854682	1220000		120000	Apr-55
11792465	0.071	12629729	837264	1220000		120000	Apr-56
11529729	0.071	12348339	818610	1220000		120000	Apr-57
11248339	0.071	12046970	798631	1220000		120000	Apr-58
10946970	0.071	11724204	777234	1220000		120000	Apr-59
10624204	0.071	11378522	754318	1220000		120000	Apr-60
10278522	0.071	11008296	729774	1220000		120000	Apr-61
9908296	0.071	10611784	703488	1220000		120000	Apr-62
9511784	0.071	10187120	675336	1220000		120000	Apr-63
9087120	0.071	9732305	645185	1220000		120000	Apr-64
8632305	0.071	9245197	612893	1220000		120000	Apr-65
8145197	0.071	8723506	578308	1220000		120000	Apr-66
7623506	0.071	8164774	541268	1220000		120000	Apr-67
7064774	0.071	7566372	501598	1220000		120000	Apr-68
6466372	0.071	6925484	459112	1220000		120000	Apr-69
5825484	0.071	6239093	413609	1220000		120000	Apr-70
5139093	0.071	5503969	364875	1220000		120000	Apr-71
4403969	0.071	4716650	Withdraw & Enjoy				Apr-72

TABLE 2:

Assuming you start depositing Rs.1,50,000/- every year in PPF Account at the age of 30 and continue it till you turn 60 years. From 61st year onward, you start withdrawing Rs.16,00,000/- p.a. and

Retirement Planning

keep depositing Rs. 1,50,000/- till the age of 80 years. You will still be left with Rs.28.60 lacs approximately when you turn 81.

It means you will have Rs.14,50,000/- every year for your monthly expenses and if your spouse is also working and he/she also starts saving only Rs.12,500/- per month, then you will have Rs.29,00,000/- every year to enjoy your second innings.

PPF DEPOSIT @ RS.12500/- pm (Rs.1,50,000/- every year from the age of 30)						
Op. Bal.	Intt. Rate	Cl.bal.	Interest	Withdrawal	Annual Dep.	Year
0	0.071	0	0	0	150000	Apr-22
150000	0.071	160650	10650	0	150000	Apr-23
310650	0.071	332706	22056	0	150000	Apr-24
482706	0.071	516978	34272	0	150000	Apr-25
666978	0.071	714334	47355	0	150000	Apr-26
864334	0.071	925701	61368	0	150000	Apr-27
1075701	0.071	1152076	76375	0	150000	Apr-28
1302076	0.071	1394523	92447	0	150000	Apr-29
1544523	0.071	1654184	109661	0	150000	Apr-30
1804184	0.071	1932281	128097	0	150000	Apr-31
2082281	0.071	2230123	147842	0	150000	Apr-32
2380123	0.071	2549111	168989	0	150000	Apr-33
2699111	0.071	2890748	191637	0	150000	Apr-34
3040748	0.071	3256641	215893	0	150000	Apr-35
3406641	0.071	3648512	241871	0	150000	Apr-36
3798512	0.071	4068206	269694	0	150000	Apr-37
4218206	0.071	4517699	299492	0	150000	Apr-38
4667699	0.071	4999105	331406	0	150000	Apr-39
5149105	0.071	5514691	365586	0	150000	Apr-40
5664691	0.071	6066884	402193	0	150000	Apr-41
6216884	0.071	6658282	441398	0	150000	Apr-42
6808282	0.071	7291669	483387	0	150000	Apr-43
7441669	0.071	7970027	528358	0	150000	Apr-44
8120027	0.071	8696548	576521	0	150000	Apr-45
8846548	0.071	9474653	628104	0	150000	Apr-46
9624653	0.071	10308002	683350	0	150000	Apr-47

Wealth & Wellbeing

10458002	0.071	11200519	742517	0	150000	Apr-48
11350519	0.071	12156405	805886	0	150000	Apr-49
12306405	0.071	13180159	873754	0	150000	Apr-50
13330159	0.071	14276599	946440	0	150000	Apr-51
14426599	0.071	15450887	1024287	0	150000	Apr-52
15600887	0.071	16708548	1107662	1600000	150000	Apr-53
15258548	0.071	16341904	1083356	1600000	150000	Apr-54
14891904	0.071	15949228	1057324	1600000	150000	Apr-55
14499228	0.071	15528672	1029444	1600000	150000	Apr-56
14078672	0.071	15078257	999585	1600000	150000	Apr-57
13628257	0.071	14595862	967605	1600000	150000	Apr-58
13145862	0.071	14079217	933355	1600000	150000	Apr-59
12629217	0.071	13525890	896673	1600000	150000	Apr-60
12075890	0.071	12933278	857387	1600000	150000	Apr-61
11483278	0.071	12298589	815312	1600000	150000	Apr-62
10848589	0.071	11618838	770249	1600000	150000	Apr-63
10168838	0.071	10890825	721987	1600000	150000	Apr-64
9440825	0.071	10111123	670298	1600000	150000	Apr-65
8661123	0.071	9276062	614939	1600000	150000	Apr-66
7826062	0.071	8381711	555650	1600000	150000	Apr-67
6931711	0.071	7423862	492151	1600000	150000	Apr-68
5973862	0.071	6398006	424144	1600000	150000	Apr-69
4948006	0.071	5299314	351308	1600000	150000	Apr-70
3849314	0.071	4122615	273301	1600000	150000	Apr-71
2672615	0.071	2862371	Withdraw & Enjoy			Apr-72

Table 3:

Assuming you start a PPF deposit of Rs.1,50,000/- per year from the age of 35 and continue the account till you are 80 years. You can withdraw Rs.11,30,000/- every year from the 61st year onward till you turn 80 and on 81st year, close the PPF Account and you will be getting maturity proceeds of Rs. 16 lacs approximately.

(Going by the same calculations, if you deposit Rs.10,000/- per month i.e. Rs.1,20,000/- in PPF A/c. from the age of 35 years and maintain the account as above, you can withdraw Rs.9,00,000/- every

Retirement Planning

year still leaving a balance of Rs.13.42 lacs approximately at the end of 80 years.)

PPF Deposit @ 12,500/- pm (Rs.1,50,000/- p.a. every year from the age of 35)						
Op. Bal.	Intt. Rate	Cl.bal.	Interest	Withdrawal	Annual Dep.	Year
0	0.071	0	0	0	150000	Apr-22
150000	0.071	160650	10650	0	150000	Apr-23
310650	0.071	332706	22056	0	150000	Apr-24
482706	0.071	516978	34272	0	150000	Apr-25
666978	0.071	714334	47355	0	150000	Apr-26
864334	0.071	925701	61368	0	150000	Apr-27
1075701	0.071	1152076	76375	0	150000	Apr-28
1302076	0.071	1394523	92447	0	150000	Apr-29
1544523	0.071	1654184	109661	0	150000	Apr-30
1804184	0.071	1932281	128097	0	150000	Apr-31
2082281	0.071	2230123	147842	0	150000	Apr-32
2380123	0.071	2549111	168989	0	150000	Apr-33
2699111	0.071	2890748	191637	0	150000	Apr-34
3040748	0.071	3256641	215893	0	150000	Apr-35
3406641	0.071	3648512	241871	0	150000	Apr-36
3798512	0.071	4068206	269694	0	150000	Apr-37
4218206	0.071	4517699	299492	0	150000	Apr-38
4667699	0.071	4999105	331406	0	150000	Apr-39
5149105	0.071	5514691	365586	0	150000	Apr-40
5664691	0.071	6066884	402193	0	150000	Apr-41
6216884	0.071	6658282	441398	0	150000	Apr-42
6808282	0.071	7291669	483387	0	150000	Apr-43
7441669	0.071	7970027	528358	0	150000	Apr-44
8120027	0.071	8696548	576521	0	150000	Apr-45
8846548	0.071	9474653	628104	0	150000	Apr-46
9624653	0.071	10308002	683350	0	150000	Apr-47
10458002	0.071	11200519	742517	1130000	150000	Apr-48
10220519	0.071	10946175	725656	1130000	150000	Apr-49
9966175	0.071	10673773	707598	1130000	150000	Apr-50
9693773	0.071	10382030	688257	1130000	150000	Apr-51

Wealth & Wellbeing

Op. Bal.	Intt. Rate	Cl.bal.	Interest	Withdrawal	Annual Dep.	Year
9402030	0.071	10069574	667543	1130000	150000	Apr-52
9089574	0.071	9734933	645359	1130000	150000	Apr-53
8754933	0.071	9376532	621599	1130000	150000	Apr-54
8396532	0.071	8992685	596153	1130000	150000	Apr-55
8012685	0.071	8581585	568900	1130000	150000	Apr-56
7601585	0.071	8141297	539712	1130000	150000	Apr-57
7161297	0.071	7669749	508452	1130000	150000	Apr-58
6689749	0.071	7164720	474972	1130000	150000	Apr-59
6184720	0.071	6623835	439115	1130000	150000	Apr-60
5643835	0.071	6044547	400712	1130000	150000	Apr-61
5064547	0.071	5424129	359582	1130000	150000	Apr-62
4444129	0.071	4759662	315533	1130000	150000	Apr-63
3779662	0.071	4048018	268356	1130000	150000	Apr-64
3068018	0.071	3285847	217829	1130000	150000	Apr-65
2305847	0.071	2469561	163715	1130000	150000	Apr-66
1489561	0.071	1595320	Withdraw & Enjoy			Apr-67

Table 4:

Even if you open the PPF account at the age of 40 years and start depositing Rs.1,50,000/- till the age of 80, you can withdraw Rs.7,50,000/- every year till you are 80 i.e. Rs.6,00,000/- for household expenses every year for 20 years and still you will be left with Rs.24 lacs at the age of 81 years)

PPF DEPOSIT @ RS.12500/- pm (Rs.1,50,000/- every year from the age of 40)						
Op. Bal.	Intt. Rate	Cl.bal.	Interest	Withdrawal	Annual Dep.	Year
0	0.071	0	0	0	150000	Apr-22
150000	0.071	160650	10650	0	150000	Apr-23
310650	0.071	332706	22056	0	150000	Apr-24
482706	0.071	516978	34272	0	150000	Apr-25
666978	0.071	714334	47355	0	150000	Apr-26
864334	0.071	925701	61368	0	150000	Apr-27
1075701	0.071	1152076	76375	0	150000	Apr-28
1302076	0.071	1394523	92447	0	150000	Apr-29

Retirement Planning

1544523	0.071	1654184	109661	0		150000	Apr-30
1804184	0.071	1932281	128097	0		150000	Apr-31
2082281	0.071	2230123	147842	0		150000	Apr-32
2380123	0.071	2549111	168989	0		150000	Apr-33
2699111	0.071	2890748	191637	0		150000	Apr-34
3040748	0.071	3256641	215893	0		150000	Apr-35
3406641	0.071	3648512	241871	0		150000	Apr-36
3798512	0.071	4068206	269694	0		150000	Apr-37
4218206	0.071	4517699	299492	0		150000	Apr-38
4667699	0.071	4999105	331406	0		150000	Apr-39
5149105	0.071	5514691	365586	0		150000	Apr-40
5664691	0.071	6066884	402193	0		150000	Apr-41
6216884	0.071	6658282	441398	0		150000	Apr-42
6808282	0.071	7291669	483387	750000		150000	Apr-43
6691669	0.071	7166777	475108	750000		150000	Apr-44
6566777	0.071	7033018	466241	750000		150000	Apr-45
6433018	0.071	6889762	456744	750000		150000	Apr-46
6289762	0.071	6736334	446573	750000		150000	Apr-47
6136334	0.071	6572013	435679	750000		150000	Apr-48
5972013	0.071	6396026	424012	750000		150000	Apr-49
5796026	0.071	6207543	411517	750000		150000	Apr-50
5607543	0.071	6005678	398135	750000		150000	Apr-51
5405678	0.071	5789481	383803	750000		150000	Apr-52
5189481	0.071	5557934	368453	750000		150000	Apr-53
4957934	0.071	5309947	352013	750000		150000	Apr-54
4709947	0.071	5044352	334406	750000		150000	Apr-55
4444352	0.071	4759901	315549	750000		150000	Apr-56
4159901	0.071	4455254	295353	750000		150000	Apr-57
3855254	0.071	4128976	273723	750000		150000	Apr-58
3528976	0.071	3779533	250557	750000		150000	Apr-59
3179533	0.071	3405280	225747	750000		150000	Apr-60
2805280	0.071	3004455	199175	750000		150000	Apr-61
2404455	0.071	2575171	Withdraw & Enjoy				Apr-62

Wealth & Wellbeing

Table 5:

Assuming you are now 45 years of age and wish to open a PPF Account. Please open it immediately as with the deposit of Rs.1,50,000/- p.a. up to the age of 80 years will allow you withdrawal of Rs.7,80,000/- every year from the age of 61 till you are 80 still leaving a balance of Rs.13.60 lacs approximately during maturity.

PPF Deposit of Rs.1,50,000/- every year from the age of 45 years)						
Op. Bal.	Intt. Rate	Cl.bal.	Interest	Withdrawal	Annual Dep.	Year
0	0.071	0	0	0	150000	Apr-22
150000	0.071	160650	10650	0	150000	Apr-23
310650	0.071	332706	22056	0	150000	Apr-24
482706	0.071	516978	34272	0	150000	Apr-25
666978	0.071	714334	47355	0	150000	Apr-26
864334	0.071	925701	61368	0	150000	Apr-27
1075701	0.071	1152076	76375	0	150000	Apr-28
1302076	0.071	1394523	92447	0	150000	Apr-29
1544523	0.071	1654184	109661	0	150000	Apr-30
1804184	0.071	1932281	128097	0	150000	Apr-31
2082281	0.071	2230123	147842	0	150000	Apr-32
2380123	0.071	2549111	168989	0	150000	Apr-33
2699111	0.071	2890748	191637	0	150000	Apr-34
3040748	0.071	3256641	215893	0	150000	Apr-35
3406641	0.071	3648512	241871	0	150000	Apr-36
3798512	0.071	4068206	269694	0	150000	Apr-37
4218206	0.071	4517699	299492	0	150000	Apr-38
4667699	0.071	4999105	331406	0	150000	Apr-39
5149105	0.071	5514691	365586	0	150000	Apr-40
5664691	0.071	6066884	402193	0	150000	Apr-41
6216884	0.071	6658282	441398	0	150000	Apr-42
6808282	0.071	7291669	483387	780000	150000	Apr-43
6661669	0.071	7134647	472978	780000	150000	Apr-44
6504647	0.071	6966477	461829	780000	150000	Apr-45
6336477	0.071	6786366	449889	780000	150000	Apr-46
6156366	0.071	6593467	437101	780000	150000	Apr-47

5963467	0.071	6386873	423406	780000	150000	Apr-48
5756873	0.071	6165611	408738	780000	150000	Apr-49
5535611	0.071	5928638	393028	780000	150000	Apr-50
5298638	0.071	5674841	376203	780000	150000	Apr-51
5044841	0.071	5403025	358183	780000	150000	Apr-52
4773025	0.071	5111909	338884	780000	150000	Apr-53
4481909	0.071	4800124	318215	780000	150000	Apr-54
4170124	0.071	4466203	296078	780000	150000	Apr-55
3836203	0.071	4108573	272370	780000	150000	Apr-56
3478573	0.071	3725551	246978	780000	150000	Apr-57
3095551	0.071	3315335	219784	780000	150000	Apr-58
2685335	0.071	2875994	190659	780000	150000	Apr-59
2245994	0.071	2405459	159465	780000	150000	Apr-60
1775459	0.071	1901516	126057	780000	150000	Apr-61
1271516	0.071	1361794	Withdraw & Enjoy			Apr-62

It is advisable to open a PPF account even if you are nearing retirement or even 60 years of age. We shall discuss the same in the chapter for Senior Citizen Retirement Plan.

3. NPS Account:

My third choice for retirement planning at a younger age is NPS Account. We have discussed NPS Scheme. On an indicative basis, if you deposit Rs.5,000/- per month from the age of 30 years, on maturity i.e. at retirement, you will get around Rs.91.50 lacs assuming a 9% rate of return. Similarly, for the same investment, if started from the age of 35 years, you will get around Rs.56 lacs, from the age of 40 years around Rs.33 lacs, and from the age of 45 years around 19 lacs with the above assumption. However, a minimum of 40% of the maturity proceeds must be used for purchasing an annuity and the balance shall be paid to you as a lump sum. Further, an NPS account can be maintained till the age of 65 years.

Therefore, it is always advisable to open the NPS Account as early as possible to reap the benefit of higher returns. Moreover, any amount can be deposited in NPS Account as already explained.

4. Mutual Funds:

Mutual funds are considered one of the best investment options for people who can take risk of investing in equities but either due to lack of knowledge or time or patience, do not invest directly in equity shares. Mutual Funds are a better investment option because they have a large variety of schemes to suit your need as per your risk appetite, low transaction costs, and tax benefits besides they are managed by professional managers.

Equity mutual funds may give you an average 12% return p.a. in the long run whereas balance funds can also give an average return of 10% annually in the long term. For low-risk category individuals, investing in Debt Funds also is a good option. The best strategy for retirement planning through mutual funds is going via the SIP route.

5. Equities:

I have kept equities as my last priority although stocks have the potential to appreciate over the period. It is also a fact that equities have outperformed most other forms of investments in the long term. However, selecting the blue-chip companies and staying invested in them for a long time is a job full of patience and most of the investors fall prey to slight ups and downs in the market thus failing their retirement plan.

There are other investment options also available such as investing in real estate, gold/silver/precious metals, etc. as discussed in the book.

Once you have built up a retirement corpus, your main job is over. The next step is to deploy your maturity proceeds in safe schemes with guaranteed returns. We shall discuss the same in the Senior Citizen Financial Planning chapter.

30.
FINANCIAL PLANNING FOR SENIOR CITIZENS

If you are a salaried employee and reaching the retirement age, you will be getting a substantial amount as Provident Fund accumulation, Gratuity, Leave Encashment, and other terminal benefits as prevailing in your organization besides your savings. If you are self-employed, you must have created a retirement corpus by investing in various schemes.

Due to increased life expectancy, many persons are scared of 'retirement' as they always feel that their investments may not be sufficient to take care of their financial needs for another 20-25 years.

During my Financial Planning sessions for retiring employees in my Company and many other Public Sector Enterprises where I took such sessions for employees reaching the age of superannuation, my opening remark was "I guarantee you that you will be able to enjoy your second innings maintaining your current standard of living or maybe better and also leave behind good amount of money for your children".

Since most of my participants were technocrats, though experts in their domain but not having sufficient investment knowledge except what they came to know from their colleagues, friends, or agents/advisors, they were not ready to believe me. However, I have not only explained to them the various investment options and how to invest, what to invest, etc. but done Financial Planning for many participants based on their inputs e.g. their monthly expenditure requirement (of course keeping in mind the effect of inflation as we are doing planning for the next 20 years), their liabilities e.g. children's education, daughter's marriage (how much money will be required and when it will be required), existing loans, if any. Whether they are living in their house/flat or rent outgo shall be there, etc. besides seeking details of their retirement corpus, balance in their PPF Account(s), etc. I am happy that most of them are living a happy and prosperous life without any financial worries.

Based on my above experience, we shall try and understand through excel-sheets about various options where you can safely put your retirement proceeds. The investment options suggested hereunder and priorities are based on my experience of creating a financial plan for hundreds of my friends as mentioned above and my personal choice. However, you may consider them as per your priorities and understanding.

1. Your first choice should be Public Provident Fund (PPF). If you are maintaining a PPF account, please continue operating it for another 20 years. You should have a PPF account in the name of your spouse also. If you have PPF Accounts for yourself and your spouse, you will need Rs.3 lakh every year for investing in a PPF account. However, if you don't have PPF Account, although it is late, you can still consider opening the PPF Accounts for regular income from the 70th year onwards as explained in the example.
2. As we are considering payment of Rs. 1.5 lakh for the next 20 years, you need to invest the required amount in FD/NSC from your retirement corpus as explained in the table below to ensure that you get Rs.1.5 lakh before 5th April every year. In case, you are operating a PPF account for your spouse also, you have to accordingly plan for his/her investment in the PPF account for the next 20 years.
3. Your second choice should be investing Rs.15 lakh in Pradhan Mantri Vaya Vandana Yojana (PMVVY) as it will guarantee you a regular income for the next 10 years with utmost safety. If your spouse also is a senior citizen, you may invest Rs.15 lakh in her name also.
4. Your third choice should be investing Rs.15 lakh in Senior Citizen Savings Scheme (SCSS). Here also, if your spouse is also a senior citizen, invest Rs.15 lakh in his/her name also.
5. The next will be to deposit Rs. 5-10 lakh in GOI Bonds as per your retirement corpus which will generate regular income for

Financial Planning For Senior Citizens

you for the next seven years. If you have more amounts to deposit in GOI Bonds, try to invest in your spouse's name also.

6. Your next choice should be investment in the Post office Monthly Income Scheme (MIS). In MIS, the maximum investment limit is Rs.4.5 lakh in the individual name. However, you can open an account with your spouse and deposit Rs. 9 lakh in your MIS Account. Open a savings account also in the same post office and give an application for the transfer of monthly income from the MIS scheme to your savings account. Attached with this savings account, open a recurring account for the same duration i.e. 5 years from where the proceeds shall be transferred to your recurring account, if requested.

7. Your next choice should be investing in Fixed Deposits as banks give higher interest to Senior Citizens. Many small finance banks are giving comparatively higher interest rates than nationalized and big banks e.g. Jana Bank is giving interest of 7.55% to senior citizens for deposits from 1 to 5 years from January 2022. You can safely invest small amounts i.e. up to Rs. 5 lakh in such small banks as your deposit is insured by DICGC in scheduled commercial banks.

8. Your next choice should be to invest in debt funds in which you can invest safely as they may give you a little less return as compared to equity funds but they are relatively much safer. However, the selection of a good fund is a task that has to be performed with utmost care. If required, you may seek the help of an advisor in this regard.

9. As we are talking of financial planning for senior citizens, my last choice will be equity funds or direct investment in equity shares. Undoubtedly there is the scope of higher returns as compared to any other option mentioned above but there are many uncertainties associated with such investment and therefore it is risky. Moreover, investment in equities yields better returns if kept for a longer period and it may be seen as leaving a legacy.

10. There are several other options available e.g. annuity schemes, investment in commodities, etc. but these may not be very beneficial at this stage of life. We shall discuss step-by-step retirement planning for persons nearing retirement in the next chapter.

31.
STEPS TO RETIREMENT PLANNING & ILLUSTRATIONS

It is a fact that learning comes much faster with practical examples. I have therefore tried to translate the available investment options into real-life situations by way of examples illustrating different situations, circumstances, requirements, expectations, etc. of individuals and how to invest their 'retirement corpus' i.e. total savings to ensure regular income till they are alive and fulfill their aspirations of leading a safe, secure and tension free life in their golden years i.e. 'retired life'.

You can also easily do your retirement planning by following under-mentioned steps:

i) List down all your liabilities as on the date of retirement e.g. repayment of home-loan/construction/renovation of house/flat, children education, daughter's marriage, other loans, if any, etc. Write down tentative dates when you have to meet these liabilities. For example, if you are planning marriage of your daughter after two years, indicate a tentative date/month.

ii) Make a budget of your monthly expenses including requirement of regular medicines, tax liabilities, etc. We generally tend to keep it on higher side but my advice is to make your budget realistic and avoid temptation of keeping extra money in hand.

iii) Calculate your retirement corpus i.e. the money in your hand as on the date of retirement which will include your gratuity, EPF, leave encashment, other terminal benefits, your savings, your LIC policies and their date of maturity, etc.

iv) Balance in PPF Account and date when opened as withdrawals from PPF account can be after seven years as explained, if you have PPF account.

v) If you have PPF Account for your spouse also, balance in his/her account as on the date of retirement.

vi) If your spouse is also working, try to make financial planning for him/her separately following above steps.

vii) Copy one of the illustrations from the book which is near your requirements in excel sheet on your laptop/computer and change the figures based on the list you have prepared.

viii) Please note that the investments given in the illustrations are only examples and it's your money which you are planning to invest, so invest it wisely as per prevailing interest rates and your requirements, keeping in view the duration of the scheme, lock-in period, etc.

ILLUSTRATION – 1

Mr. Sharma is retiring on 31st March 2022 on attaining the age of 60 years. He has a total retirement corpus of Rs.60 lacs plus Rs.15 lacs balance in his PPF account which he opened 10 years ago.

He lives in his house with his spouse, His children are well settled and he doesn't have any liabilities. He requires Rs.35,000/- per month currently (inflation has to be considered in the next 20 years) towards monthly expenses and Rs. 50,000/- every year for vacations at least for another 20 years.

Tentative Retirement financial planning for Mr. Sharma will be as under:-

SL.NO.	PARTICULARS	INVESTMENT	MATURITY AMOUNT	PERIOD
I	RETIREMENT PROCEEDS 1.4.2022	5000000		
II	INVESTMENTS:			
1	PMVVY SCHEME (LIC)	1450000		
	You will get Rs.1,11,000/- every year for 10 years		111000 p.a.	From Apr.23
2	PO-SENIOR CITIZEN SAVINGS SCHEME	1500000	111000 p.a.	for 8 years
	Deposit for 5 years			
	Income Rs.27,750/- per quarter			
	(Please extend for 3 years after maturity)			
	(Thereafter make FD of this amount)			
3	GOI (TAXABLE) BONDS-2020	1000000	71500 p.a.	for 7 years
	(preferably buy in two names)			
4	FDs for DEPOSIT IN PPF A/C			

	FD FOR 1 YEAR (MAT. 2nd April)	140000	150060	
	FD FOR 2 YEAR (MAT. 2nd April)	135000	155099	
	FD FOR 3 YEAR (MAT. 2nd April)	125000	153930	
	FD FOR 4 YEAR (MAT. 2nd April)	115000	151792	
	NSC (VIII ISSUE)	110000	152844	
	(Intt. @ 7% p.a. considered)			
5	FDs for HOUSEHOLD EXPENSES			
5.1	FD FOR 1 YEAR (MAT. 2nd April)	170000	182216	
5.2	FD FOR 2 YEAR (MAT. 2nd April)	160000	183821	
5.3	FD FOR 3 YEAR (MAT. 2nd April)	150000	184716	
5.4	FD FOR 4 YEAR (MAT. 2nd April)	140000	184790	
5.5	FD FOR 5 YEAR (MAT. 2nd April)	130000	183921	
	(Intt. @ 7% p.a. considered)			
6	DEPOSIT IN PPF A/C (APR.22)	150000		
7	BALANCE IN SAVINGS A/C FOR 1st YEAR EXPENSES	470000		
	(FLEXI ACCOUNT OF SBI)			
8	RETIREMENT PARTY / PILGRIMAGE	55000		
	(or keep in a savings account for exigencies)			
	HOUSE HOLD EXPENSES			
1	FOR THE YEAR 2022		470000	
	(from savings a/c at Sl. No. 7)			

		Monthly expenses 35000/- per month +			
		For Travel/ Vactions - Rs.50,000/-			
	2	From 1.4.23 to 31.3.2028			
		from PMVVY Scheme Rs.1,11,000			
		from SCSS Scheme Rs.1,11,000			
		from GOI Bonds Rs.71,500			
		from FD at Sl. 5 Rs.1,82,000		475500	
		Monthly expenses @ Rs.39,625/- p.m.			
	3	From 1.4.28 onwards			
		from PMVVY Scheme* Rs.1,11,000			
		from SCSS Scheme* Rs.1,11,000			
		from GOI Bonds* Rs. 71,500			
		From PPF A/c. Rs.3,50,000**		643500	***
		* assuming re-investing in same/similar schemes			
		** Rs.1,50,000/- kept for deposit in PPF (Till 80 yrs)			
		*** Amount received every year will be more than			
		your requirement. Keep in Flexi savings a/c and LIVE CASH RICH			
	4	At 81 years of age, you will be left with Rs. 48 lacs			
		(14.50 PMVVY+15 SCSS+ 10 GOI Bonds+8.5 PPF)			

PPF DEPOSIT MR. SHARMA (FOR NEXT 20 YEARS)						
Op. Bal.	Intt. Rate	Cl.bal.	Interest	Withdrawal	Annual Dep. (Before 5th Apr)	Year
1500000	0.071	1606500	106500	0	150000	Apr-22
1756500	0.071	1881211	124711		150000	Apr-23
2031211	0.071	2175427	144216		150000	Apr-24
2325427	0.071	2490532	165105		150000	Apr-25
2640532	0.071	2828010	187478		150000	Apr-26
2978010	0.071	3189448	211438		150000	Apr-27
3339448	0.071	3576549	237101	500000	150000	Apr-28
3226549	0.071	3455633	229085	500000	150000	Apr-29
3105633	0.071	3326133	220500	500000	150000	Apr-30
2976133	0.071	3187438	211305	500000	150000	Apr-31
2837438	0.071	3038896	201458	500000	150000	Apr-32
2688896	0.071	2879808	190911	500000	150000	Apr-33
2529808	0.071	2709424	179616	500000	150000	Apr-34
2359424	0.071	2526943	167519	500000	150000	Apr-35
2176943	0.071	2331506	154563	500000	150000	Apr-36
1981506	0.071	2122192	140687	500000	150000	Apr-37
1772192	0.071	1898018	125826	500000	150000	Apr-38
1548018	0.071	1657927	109909	500000	150000	Apr-39
1307927	0.071	1400790	92863	500000	150000	Apr-40
1050790	0.071	1125396	74606	500000	150000	Apr-41
775396	0.071	830449	55053			Apr-42

ILLUSTRATION – 2

Let's assume Mr. Pandey is going to retire on 31st March 2022 on attaining the age of 60 years. He has a total retirement corpus of Rs.90 lacs plus Rs.10 lacs balance in his PPF & Rs.10 lakh in his wife's PPF account which they opened 5 years ago.

He lives in his house with his spouse, His children are well settled and he doesn't have any liabilities except a balance home loan of Rs. 5 Lakh which he wishes to clear. He requires Rs.50,000/- per month currently as he has to take care of his aged parents also. He is always worried that he may be requiring more money in the coming years for the medical expenses of his parents and to beat inflation. He requires Rs.50,000/- for travel expenses every year to meet his children/vacation.

Tentative Retirement financial planning for Mr. Pandey will be as under:-

SL.NO.	PARTICULARS	INVESTMENT	MATURITY AMOUNT	PERIOD
I	RETIREMENT PROCEEDS 1.4.2022	9000000		
II	RE-PAYMENT OF HOME LOAN	500000		
III	INVESTMENTS:			
1	PMVVY SCHEME (LIC)	1450000		
	You will get Rs.1,11,000/- every year for 10 yrs		111000 p.a.	From Apr.23
2	PO-SENIOR CITIZEN SAVINGS SCHEME	1500000	111000 p.a.	for 8 years
	Deposit for 5 years			
	Income Rs.27,750/- per quarter			
	(Please extend for 3 years after maturity)			
	(Thereafter make FD of this amount)			

Steps To Retirement Planning & Illustrations

3	GOI (TAXABLE) BONDS-2020	1000000	71500 p.a.	for 7 years
	Self-name			
4	GOI (TAXABLE) BONDS-2020	1000000	71500 p.a.	for 7 years
	Preferably in Spouse Name			
5	PPF DEPOSIT (SELF) - APRIL 22	150000		
6	PPF DEPOSIT (WIFE) - APRIL 22	150000		
7	FDs for DEPOSIT IN PPF A/C (SELF)			
	FD FOR 1 YEAR (MAT. 2nd April)	140000	150060	
	FD FOR 2 YEAR (MAT. 2nd April)	135000	155099	
	FD FOR 3 YEAR (MAT. 2nd April)	125000	153930	
	FD FOR 4 YEAR (MAT. 2nd April)	115000	151792	
	FD FOR 5 YEAR (MAT. 2nd April)	110000	152844	
	(Intt. @ 7% p.a. considered)			
8	FDs for DEPOSIT IN PPF A/C (WIFE)			
	FD FOR 1 YEAR (MAT. 2nd April)	140000	150060	
	FD FOR 2 YEAR (MAT. 2nd April)	135000	155099	
	FD FOR 3 YEAR (MAT. 2nd April)	125000	153930	
	FD FOR 4 YEAR (MAT. 2nd April)	115000	151792	
	FD FOR 5 YEAR (MAT. 2nd April)	110000	152844	
9	FDs for HOUSEHOLD EXPENSES			
9.1	FD FOR 1 YEAR (MAT. 2nd April)	280000	300121	

Wealth & Wellbeing

9.2	FD FOR 2 YEAR (MAT. 2nd April)	265000	304454	
9.3	FD FOR 3 YEAR (MAT. 2nd April)	250000	307860	
9.4	FD FOR 4 YEAR (MAT. 2nd April)	235000	310183	
9.5	FD FOR 5 YEAR (MAT. 2nd April)	220000	311251	
	(Intt. @ 7% p.a. considered)			
	(Preferably in different banks)			
10	BALANCE IN SAVINGS A/C	650000		
	(preferably in Flexi account of SBI)			
11	RETIREMENT PARTY / PILGRIMAGE	100000		
	(or keep in a savings account for exigencies)			
	HOUSE-HOLD EXPENSES			
1	FOR THE YEAR 2022 (1.4.22 to 31.3.23)			
	(from savings a/c at Sl. No. 10)			
	Monthly expenses 50,000/- per month +		650000	
	For Travel/ Vactions - Rs.50,000/-			
2	From 1.4.23 to 31.3.2028			
	from PMVVY Scheme Rs.1,11,000			
	from SCSS Scheme Rs.1,11,000			
	from GOI Bonds Rs.1,43,000			
	from FD at Sl. 9* Rs.3,00,000		665000	
	*(amount will be increasing every year)			

Steps To Retirement Planning & Illustrations

3	From 1.4.28 onwards			
	from PMVVY Scheme* Rs.1,11,000			
	from SCSS Scheme* Rs.1,11,000			
	from GOI Bonds* Rs.1,43,000			
	From PPF A/c.(self) Rs.2,25,000*		815000	***
	From PPF A/c.(spouse) Rs.2,25,000*			
	* assuming re-investing in same such schemes			
	** Rs.1,50,000/- kept for deposit in PPF (Till 80 yrs)			
	*** Amount received every year will be more than			
	your requirement. Keep in Flexi savings a/c and LIVE CASH RICH			
4	At 81 years of age, you will be left with			
	Rs.64 lacs approx (14.50 PMVVY+15 SCSS+20 GOI Bonds+14.5 PPF)			
	ENJOY TILL YOU ARE ALIVE AND LEAVE BALANCE FOR CHILDREN			

PPF DEPOSIT - Mr. PANDEY (FOR NEXT 20 YEARS)						
Op. Bal.	Intt. Rate	Cl.bal.	Interest	Withdrawal	Annual Dep. (Before 5th Apr)	Year
1000000	0.071	1071000	71000	0	150000	Apr-22
1221000	0.071	1307691	86691		150000	Apr-23
1457691	0.071	1561187	103496		150000	Apr-24
1711187	0.071	1832681	121494		150000	Apr-25
1982681	0.071	2123451	140770		150000	Apr-26
2273451	0.071	2434866	161415	375000	150000	Apr-27
2209866	0.071	2366766	156900	375000	150000	Apr-28
2141766	0.071	2293831	152065	375000	150000	Apr-29
2068831	0.071	2215718	146887	375000	150000	Apr-30
1990718	0.071	2132059	141341	375000	150000	Apr-31
1907059	0.071	2042460	135401	375000	150000	Apr-32
1817460	0.071	1946500	129040	375000	150000	Apr-33
1721500	0.071	1843726	122226	375000	150000	Apr-34
1618726	0.071	1733655	114929	375000	150000	Apr-35
1508655	0.071	1615770	107114	375000	150000	Apr-36
1390770	0.071	1489514	98745	375000	150000	Apr-37
1264514	0.071	1354295	89780	375000	150000	Apr-38
1129295	0.071	1209475	80180	375000	150000	Apr-39
984475	0.071	1054372	69898	375000	150000	Apr-40
829372	0.071	888258	58885	375000	150000	Apr-41
663258	0.071	710349	47091			Apr-42

The same Statement shall be there for Ms. Pandey (PPF Account)

ILLUSTRATION – 3

Let's assume Mr. Chawla is going to retire on 31st March 2022 on attaining the age of 60 years. He has a total retirement corpus of Rs.85 lacs plus Rs.20 lacs balance in his PPF account which he opened 12 years ago.

He lives in his house with his spouse. His only daughter is a software engineer and working in a reputed IT firm. Mr. Chawla plans to marry her next year. He has some jewelry etc. already made for her but requires another around Rs.15 lacs more, which he plans to arrange from his retirement proceeds. He requires Rs.40,000/- per month for household expenses and is confident that this amount will be sufficient to take care of all his needs. However, he is also worried about the rising cost of living.

Tentative Retirement financial planning for Mr. Chawla will be as under:-

SL.NO.	PARTICULARS	INVESTMENT	MATURITY AMOUNT	
I	RETIREMENT PROCEEDS 1.4.2022	8500000		
II	INVESTMENT:			
1	FD for daughter's marriage	1500000	1607789	
	after one year			
	(preferably in nationalized bank only and			
	in two/three parts)			
2	PMVVY SCHEME (LIC)	1450000		
	You will get Rs.1,11,000/- every year for 10 years		111000 p.a.	From Apr.23
3	PO-SENIOR CITIZEN SAVINGS SCHEME	1500000	111000 p.a.	for 8 years
	Deposit for 5 years			
	Income Rs.27,750/- per quarter			
	(Please extend for 3 years after maturity)			

	(Thereafter make FD of this amount)			
4	GOI (TAXABLE) BONDS-2020 (self name)	1000000	71500 p.a.	for 7 years
5	GOI (TAXABLE) BONDS-2020 (spouse name)	1000000	71500 p.a.	for 7 years
6	PPF DEPOSIT (SELF) - APRIL 22	150000		
7	FDs for DEPOSIT IN PPF A/C (SELF)			
	FD FOR 1 YEAR (MAT. 2nd April)	140000	150060	
	FD FOR 2 YEAR (MAT. 2nd April)	135000	155099	
	FD FOR 3 YEAR (MAT. 2nd April)	125000	153930	
	FD FOR 4 YEAR (MAT. 2nd April)	115000	151792	
	FD FOR 5 YEAR (MAT. 2nd April)	110000	152844	
	(Intt. @ 7% p.a. considered)			
8	FDs for HOUSEHOLD EXPENSES (preferably in different banks)			
8.1	FD FOR 1 YEAR (MAT. 2nd April)	165000	176857	
8.2	FD FOR 2 YEAR (MAT. 2nd April)	155000	178077	
8.3	FD FOR 3 YEAR (MAT. 2nd April)	145000	178559	
8.4	FD FOR 4 YEAR (MAT. 2nd April)	135000	178190	
8.5	FD FOR 5 YEAR (MAT. 2nd April)	125000	176847	
	(Intt. @ 7% p.a. considered)			
9	BALANCE IN SAVINGS A/C	540000		
	(preferably in Flexi account of SBI)			

Steps To Retirement Planning & Illustrations

10	RETIREMENT PARTY			
1	HOUSE HOLD EXPENSES: FOR THE YEAR 2022 (1.4.22 to 31.3.23)			
	(from savings a/c at Sl. No. 10)			
	Monthly expenses @ Rs. 41,500/- per month		500000	
2	From 1.4.23 to 31.3.2028			
	from PMVVY Scheme Rs.1,11,000			
	from SCSS Scheme Rs.1,11,000			
	from GOI Bonds Rs.1,43,000			
	from FD at Sl. 9 Rs.1,76,000		541000	
	Monthly expenses @ 45,000/- per month			
3	From 1.4.28 onwards			
	from PMVVY Scheme* Rs.1,11,000			
	from SCSS Scheme* Rs.1,11,000			
	from GOI Bonds* Rs.1,43,000			
	From PPF A/c.(self) Rs.3,75,000**		740000	
	* assuming re-investing in same such schemes			
	** Rs.1,50,000/- kept for deposit in PPF (Till 80 yrs)			
	Monthly expenses @ Rs. 61,600/- per month			
4	At 81 years of age, you will be left with Rs.58 lacs approx ((14.50 PMVVY+15 SCSS+20 GOI Bonds+8.5 PPF)			

PPF DEPOSIT Mr. CHAWLA (FOR NEXT 20 YEARS)

Op. Bal.	Intt. Rate	Cl.bal.	Interest	Withdrawal	Annual Dep. (Before 5th Apr)	Year
2000000	0.071	2142000	142000	0	150000	Apr-22
2292000	0.071	2454732	162732		150000	Apr-23
2604732	0.071	2789667	184936		150000	Apr-24
2939667	0.071	3148384	208716		150000	Apr-25
3298384	0.071	3532568	234185		150000	Apr-26
3682568	0.071	3944031	261462	525000	150000	Apr-27
3569031	0.071	3822431	253401	525000	150000	Apr-28
3447431	0.071	3692199	244767	525000	150000	Apr-29
3317199	0.071	3552720	235521	525000	150000	Apr-30
3177720	0.071	3403337	225618	525000	150000	Apr-31
3028337	0.071	3243349	215012	525000	150000	Apr-32
2868349	0.071	3072002	203653	525000	150000	Apr-33
2697002	0.071	2888489	191487	525000	150000	Apr-34
2513489	0.071	2691946	178457	525000	150000	Apr-35
2316946	0.071	2481449	164503	525000	150000	Apr-36
2106449	0.071	2256007	149558	525000	150000	Apr-37
1881007	0.071	2014558	133551	525000	150000	Apr-38
1639558	0.071	1755967	116408	525000	150000	Apr-39
1380967	0.071	1479015	98049	525000	150000	Apr-40
1104015	0.071	1182400	78385	525000	150000	Apr-41
807400	0.071	864725	57325			Apr-42

Steps To Retirement Planning & Illustrations

ILLUSTRATION – 4

Let's assume Mr. Ramesh with his limited income has given the best education to his two daughters and married them also nicely. Both the girls are now enjoying happy married life. Mr. Ramesh is going to be 65 years of age in March 2022 and wishes to retire from the firm where he is working for the last 40 years. He lives in his parental house with his wife who is now 62 years. Both the spouse believe in simple living and they will be more than happy if they get Rs.25,000/- to 30,000/- per month to meet their monthly expenditure including exigencies as they do not have any other liability. Mr. Ramesh has a total retirement corpus of Rs.55 lakh only which is available for investment.

Tentative Retirement financial planning for Mr. Ramesh will be as under:-

SL.NO.	PARTICULARS	INVESTMENT	MATURITY AMOUNT	
I	RETIREMENT PROCEEDS 1.4.2022	5500000		
II	INVESTMENTS:			
1	PMVVY SCHEME (LIC) - SELF	1450000		
	You will get Rs.1,11,000/- every year for 10 years		111000 p.a.	From Apr.23
2	PMVVY SCHEME (LIC) - WIFE	1450000		
	You will get Rs.1,11,000/- every year for 10 years		111000 p.a.	From Apr.23
3	PO-SENIOR CITIZEN SAVINGS SCHEME-SELF	1000000	74000 p.a.	
	Deposit for 5 years			
	Income Rs.18,500/- per quarter			

Wealth & Wellbeing

	(Thereafter make 10 FDs for this amount)			
4	PO-SENIOR CITIZEN SAVINGS SCHEME-WIFE	1000000	74000 p.a.	
	Deposit for 5 years			
	Income Rs.18,500/- per quarter			
	(Thereafter make 10 FDs for this amount)			
5	BALANCE IN SAVINGS A/C	400000		
	(preferably in Flexi account of SBI)			
6	FD FOR EXIGENCIES/ EMERGENCY			
	FD for 3 year	50000	61572	
	FD for 4 year	50000	65996	
	FD for 5 year	50000	70739	
	FD for 5 year	50000	70739	
7	RE-INVESTMENT			
	FDs from maturity proceeds of SCSS-Rs.20 lakh			
	FD for 1 year (Mat. April 28)	245000	262605	
	FD for 2 years (Mat. April 29)	230000	264243	
	FD for 3 years (Mat. April 30)	215000	264759	
	FD for 4 years (Mat. April 31)	205000	270586	
	FD for 5 years (Mat. April 32)	195000	275882	
	FD for 6 years (Mat. April 33)	200000	303289	
	FD for 7 years (Mat. April 34)	190000	308828	
	FD for 8 years (Mat. April 35)	180000	313598	

Steps To Retirement Planning & Illustrations

	FD for 9 years (Mat. April 36)	170000	317459	
	FD for 10 year(Mat. April 37)	170000	340272	
	(interest @ 7% considered)			
	HOUSE-HOLD EXPENSES			
1	FOR THE YEAR 2022 (1.4.22 to 31.3.23)			
	(from savings a/c at Sl. No. 5)			
	Monthly expenses 30,000/- per month plus		400000	
	Rs.40,000/- in bank a/c for exigencies			
2	From 1.4.23 to 31.3.2028			
	from PMVVY Scheme-self* Rs.1,11,000			
	from PMVVY Scheme-wife* Rs.1,11,000			
	from SCSS Scheme-self Rs. 74,000			
	from SCSS Scheme-wife Rs. 74,000		370000	
	Monthly expenses @ Rs.30,000/-p.m +			
	Rs.10,000/- for exigencies			
	* assuming re-investing in same/similar scheme			
3	From 1.4.28 to 31.3.2038			
	from PMVVY Scheme-self Rs.1,11,000			
	from PMVVY Scheme-wife Rs.1,11,000			
	from FD at Sl. No. 7 Rs.2,60,000**		482000	
	Monthly expenses @ Rs. Rs.40,000/- p.m.			
	** This amount will be increasing every year			

Wealth & Wellbeing

	YOU WILL ALWAYS BE CASH RICH			
4	At 81 years of age, you will still be having			
	Regular income of Rs.2,22,000/- p.a. plus			
	sufficient balance in your bank account.			
	ENJOY TILL YOU ARE ALIVE & LEAVE BALANCE			
	FOR DAUGHTERS			

ILLUSTRATION – 5

Let's assume, Mr. Raman is going to retire from services on 31st March 2022 on attaining the age of superannuation. His parents live in a village but Mr. Raman is not in a position to go back to the village as his wife needs regular medical care. He has built a beautiful home at the metro and his children are well settled abroad. However, he is sending Rs.10,000/- per month regularly to his parent for a long although they have land and property in the village. Mr. Raman wants to continue sending this amount even after his retirement. His total retirement corpus is 1.15 crores and he has Rs.25,00,000/- balance in his PPF account, which he opened 9 years back. His estimated monthly expenditure is Rs. 60,000/- including medical expenses for his wife's treatment who is also a senior citizen. Both husband/wife wish to travel abroad and meet their children/grandchildren every alternate year for which Rs.2,00,000/- is required.

Tentative Retirement financial planning for Mr. Raman will be as under:-

SL.NO.	PARTICULARS	INVESTMENT	MATURITY AMOUNT	PERIOD
I	RETIREMENT PROCEEDS 1.4.2022	11500000		
II	INVESTMENTS:			
1	PMVVY SCHEME (LIC) - SELF	1450000		
	You will get Rs.1,11,000/- every year		111000 p.a.	for 10 yrs
	for 10 years			from Apr.23
2	PMVVY SCHEME (LIC) - WIFE	1450000		
	You will get Rs.1,11,000/- every year		111000 p.a.	for 10 yrs
	for 10 years			from Apr.23

3	PO-SENIOR CITIZEN SAVINGS SCHEME-SELF	1500000	111000 p.a.	for 8 years
	Deposit for 5 years			
	Income Rs.18,500/- per quarter			
	(Extend for 3 years & thereafter re-invest)			
4	PO-SENIOR CITIZEN SAVINGS SCHEME-WIFE	1500000	111000 p.a.	for 8 years
	Deposit for 5 years			
	Income Rs.18,500/- per quarter			
	(Extend for 3 years & thereafter re-invest)			
5	GOI (TAXABLE) BONDS-2020 - SELF	1000000	71500 p.a.	for 7 years
6	GOI (TAXABLE) BONDS-2020 - WIFE	1000000	71500 p.a.	for 7 years
7	PPF ACCOUNT (APRIL 2022)	150000		
8	FD FOR PPF DEPOSITS (NEXT 5 YEARS)			
	FD FOR 1 YEAR	140000	150060	
	FD FOR 2 YEAR	135000	155099	
	FD FOR 3 YEAR	125000	153930	
	FD FOR 4 YEAR	115000	151792	
	FD FOR 5 YEAR	110000	155626	
9	FD FOR HOUSEHOLD EXPENSES			
	FD FOR 1 YEAR	240000	257246	
	FD FOR 2 YEAR	225000	258498	
	FD FOR 3 YEAR	210000	258602	
	FD FOR 4 YEAR	195000	257386	
	FD FOR 5 YEAR	185000	261734	
10	BALANCE IN SAVINGS A/C	1050000		
	(preferably in Flexi account of SBI)			

11	FD FOR TOUR/ TRAVEL - ABROAD			
	FD FOR 2 YEARS	180000	206799	
	FD FOR 4 YEARS	160000	211189	
	FD FOR 6 YEARS	140000	212302	
12	FOR EXIGENCIES/ EMERGENCY			
	FD FOR 3 YEARS	100000	123144	
	FD FOR 5 YEARS	100000	141478	
13	RETIREMENT PARTY	40000		
	HOUSE-HOLD EXPENSES			
1	FOR THE YEAR 2022 (1.4.22 to 31.3.23)			
	(from savings a/c at Sl. No. 10)			
	Monthly expenses @ 60,000/- pm		720000	
	For Parents @ Rs.10,000/- pm		120000	
	For visiting children after retirement		200000	
2	From 1.4.23 to 31.3.2028			
	from PMVVY Scheme(Sl.1 &2) Rs.2,22,000		844000	
	from SCSS Scheme (Sl.3 & 4) Rs.2,22,000			
	from GOI Bonds (Sl.5 & 6) Rs.1,43,000			
	From FDs (Sl. 9) Rs.2,57,000			
	Monthly expenses @ 60,000/- pm and			
	For Parents @ Rs.10,000/- pm			
3	From 1.4.28 ONWARDS			
	from PMVVY Scheme(Sl.1 &2) Rs.2,22,000*			

	from SCSS Scheme (Sl.3 & 4) Rs.2,22,000*			
	from GOI Bonds (Sl.5 &6) Rs.1,43,000*			
	from PPF A/C Rs.6,60,000		1247000 p.a	
	Monthly expenses @ 60,000/- pm and			
	For Parents @ Rs.10,000/- pm			
	For PPF depost Rs. 1,50,000/- p.a.			
	For Tour/travel Rs. 2,00,000/-p.a.			
	*Assuming re-investment in same/			
	similar schemes on maturity			
4	At 81 years of age, you will still be having			
	approx. Rs.90 lacs to live CASH RICH			
	till you are alive & leave balance for kids.			

PPF DEPOSIT Mr. Raman (FOR NEXT 20 YEARS)						
Op. Bal.	Intt. Rate	Cl.bal.	Interest	Withdrawal	Annual Dep. (Before 5th Apr)	Year
2500000	0.071	2677500	177500	0	150000	Apr-22
2827500	0.071	3028252	200752		150000	Apr-23
3178252	0.071	3403908	225656		150000	Apr-24
3553908	0.071	3806235	252327		150000	Apr-25
3956235	0.071	4237127	280892		150000	Apr-26
4387127	0.071	4698613	311486		150000	Apr-27
4848613	0.071	5192864	344251	660000	150000	Apr-28
4682864	0.071	5015347	332483	660000	150000	Apr-29
4505347	0.071	4825226	319879	660000	150000	Apr-30
4315226	0.071	4621607	306381	660000	150000	Apr-31
4111607	0.071	4403531	291924	660000	150000	Apr-32
3893531	0.071	4169971	276440	660000	150000	Apr-33
3659971	0.071	3919829	259858	660000	150000	Apr-34
3409829	0.071	3651926	242098	660000	150000	Apr-35
3141926	0.071	3365003	223077	660000	150000	Apr-36
2855003	0.071	3057708	202705	660000	150000	Apr-37
2547708	0.071	2728595	180887	660000	150000	Apr-38
2218595	0.071	2376115	157520	660000	150000	Apr-39
1866115	0.071	1998609	132494	660000	150000	Apr-40
1488609	0.071	1594300	105691	660000	150000	Apr-41
1084300	0.071	1161285	76985			Apr-42

Wealth & Wellbeing

ILLUSTRATION – 6

Mr. Shyam is going to be 65 years old in March 2022 and wishes to retire. He has the responsibility of one differently able son and expenditure on his care/medical expenses is around Rs.8,000/- pm. His total retirement corpus is only Rs. 60 lakh. However, he opened a PPF account in his name and his wife's name five years ago and there is a balance of Rs.7 lakh each in both accounts. He doesn't have any other liability on his head but is worried about meeting his monthly estimated expenses of Rs.25,000/- to 30,000/- per month besides taking care of his son. He lives on his parental property and wishes to leave a good amount for his son even after his death.

Tentative Retirement financial planning for Mr. Shyam will be as under:-

SL.NO.	PARTICULARS	INVESTMENT	MATURITY AMOUNT	PERIOD
I	RETIREMENT PROCEEDS 1.4.2022	6000000		
II	INVESTMENTS:			
1	PMVVY SCHEME (LIC) - SELF	1450000		
	You will get Rs.1,11,000/- every year for 10 yrs		111000 p.a.	From Apr.23
2	DEPOSIT IN PPF A/C (APR.22)-SELF	150000		
3	DEPOSIT IN PPF A/C (APR.22)-WIFE	150000		
4	FDs for DEPOSIT IN PPF A/C - SELF			
	FD FOR 1 YEAR (MAT. 2nd April)	140000	150060	
	FD FOR 2 YEAR (MAT. 2nd April)	135000	155099	
	FD FOR 3 YEAR (MAT. 2nd April)	125000	153930	
	FD FOR 4 YEAR (MAT. 2nd April)	115000	151792	

	FD FOR 5 YEAR (MAT. 2nd April)	110000	155626	
	FD FOR 6 YEAR (MAT. 2nd April)	100000	151644	
5	FDs for DEPOSIT IN PPF A/C - wife			
	FD FOR 1 YEAR (MAT. 2nd April)	140000	150060	
	FD FOR 2 YEAR (MAT. 2nd April)	135000	155099	
	FD FOR 3 YEAR (MAT. 2nd April)	125000	153930	
	FD FOR 4 YEAR (MAT. 2nd April)	115000	151792	
	FD FOR 5 YEAR (MAT. 2nd April)	110000	155626	
	FD FOR 6 YEAR (MAT. 2nd April)	100000	151644	
	(Intt. @ 7% p.a. considered)			
6	SAVINGS A/C FOR 1ST YEAR EXPENSES	480000		
	(keep in Flexi savings a/c)			
7	FDs for HOUSEHOLD EXPENSES			
	FD FOR 1 YEAR (MAT. 2nd April)	345000	369791	
	FD FOR 2 YEAR (MAT. 2nd April)	325000	373387	
	FD FOR 3 YEAR (MAT. 2nd April)	300000	369432	
	FD FOR 4 YEAR (MAT. 2nd April)	280000	369580	
	FD FOR 5 YEAR (MAT. 2nd April)	265000	374916	
	FD FOR 6 YEAR (MAT. 2nd April)	245000	371528	
8	KVP (10+ YEARS)	500000	1000000	
	(re-invest in KVP for another 10 years)			
9	RETIREMENT PARTY	60000		

	(or keep in savings a/c for exigencies)			
	HOUSE-HOLD EXPENSES			
1	FOR THE YEAR 2022		470000	
	(from savings a/c at Sl. No. 6)			
	Monthly expenses Rs.30,000/- p.m.			
	For Son's care Rs.9,100/- p.m.			
2	From 1.4.23 to 31.3.2029			
	from PMVVY Scheme Rs.1,11,000			
	from FD at Sl. 7 Rs.3,70,000		481400	
	Monthly expenses @ Rs.30,000/- p.m.			
	For Son's care Rs.10,000/- p.m.			
3	From 1.4.29 to 31.3.2042			
	from PMVVY Scheme* Rs.1,11,000			
	from PPF - SELF Rs.3,50,000			
	from PPF - WIFE Rs.3,50,000		811000	
	* assuming re-investing in same/similar scheme			
	Monthly expenses Rs.32,500/- p.m.			
	For Son's care Rs.10,000/- p.m.			
	PPF Deposit Rs.3,00,000/- p.a.			
4	At 81 years of age, your total corpus will be Rs. 75 lacs approx i.e. you will leave sufficient balance for your son			

Steps To Retirement Planning & Illustrations

PPF DEPOSIT Mr. Shyam & Ms. Shyam (separately) (FOR NEXT 20 YEARS)						
Op. Bal.	Intt. Rate	Cl.bal.	Interest	Withdrawal	Annual Dep. (Before 5th Apr)	Year
700000	0.071	749700	49700	0	150000	Apr-22
899700	0.071	963579	63879		150000	Apr-23
1113579	0.071	1192643	79064		150000	Apr-24
1342643	0.071	1437970	95328		150000	Apr-25
1587970	0.071	1700716	112746		150000	Apr-26
1850716	0.071	1982116	131401		150000	Apr-27
2132116	0.071	2283497	151380		150000	Apr-28
2433497	0.071	2606275	172778	350000	150000	Apr-29
2406275	0.071	2577120	170845	350000	150000	Apr-30
2377120	0.071	2545895	168775	350000	150000	Apr-31
2345895	0.071	2512454	166558	350000	150000	Apr-32
2312454	0.071	2476638	164184	350000	150000	Apr-33
2276638	0.071	2438279	161641	350000	150000	Apr-34
2238279	0.071	2397196	158918	350000	150000	Apr-35
2197196	0.071	2353197	156001	350000	150000	Apr-36
2153197	0.071	2306074	152877	350000	150000	Apr-37
2106074	0.071	2255605	149531	350000	150000	Apr-38
2055605	0.071	2201553	145948	350000	150000	Apr-39
2001553	0.071	2143663	142110	350000	150000	Apr-40
1943663	0.071	2081663	138000	350000	150000	Apr-41
1881663	0.071	2015261	133598			Apr-42

Wealth & Wellbeing

ILLUSTRATION – 7

Mr. Mukherjee is retiring from a senior position in a private firm on attaining the age of 60 years. His children are well-settled and he has no liability on his head. His wife is also a senior citizen. He has a total retirement corpus of Rs.1.25 crores besides having Rs.30 lakh in his PPF account which he opened 20 years ago.

He lives in his flat and requires around Rs.65,000/- per month for monthly expenditure including exigencies. He plans to go on foreign vacation every year till the age of 80 years and his estimated expenditure on such vacation shall be Rs.2,00,000/- per trip.

Tentative Retirement financial planning for Mr. Mukherjee will be as under:-

SL.NO.	PARTICULARS	INVESTMENT	MATURITY AMOUNT	PERIOD
I	RETIREMENT PROCEEDS 1.4.2022	12500000		
II	INVESTMENTS:			
1	PMVVY SCHEME (LIC) - SELF	1450000		
	You will get Rs.1,11,000/- every year for 10 yrs		111000 p.a.	From Apr.23
2	PMVVY SCHEME (LIC) - WIFE	1450000		
	You will get Rs.1,11,000/- every year for 10 yrs		111000 p.a.	From Apr.23
3	PO-SENIOR CITIZEN SAVINGS SCHEME-SELF	1500000	111000 p.a.	for 8 years
	(Extend for 3 years & thereafter re-invest)			
4	PO-SENIOR CITIZEN SAVINGS SCHEME-WIFE	1500000	111000 p.a.	for 8 years
	(Extend for 3 years & thereafter re-invest)			

Steps To Retirement Planning & Illustrations

5	GOI (TAXABLE) BONDS-2020 - self	1000000	71500 p.a.	for 7 years
6	GOI (TAXABLE) BONDS-2020 - wife	1000000	71500 p.a.	for 7 years
7	PPF ACCOUNT (APRIL 2022)	150000		
8	FD FOR PPF DEPOSITS (NEXT 5 YEARS)			
8.1	FD FOR 1 YEAR	140000	150060	
8.2	FD FOR 2 YEAR	135000	155099	
8.3	FD FOR 3 YEAR	125000	153930	
8.4	FD FOR 4 YEAR	115000	151792	
8.5	FD FOR 5 YEAR	110000	155626	
9	MUTUAL FUNDS (ETF/ INDEX FUND)	1000000		
10	IN FLEXI SAVINGS A/C	1000000		
11	FD FOR HOUSEHOLD EXPENSES			
	FD FOR 1 YEAR	390000	418025	
	FD FOR 2 YEAR	365000	419342	
	FD FOR 3 YEAR	340000	418689	
	FD FOR 4 YEAR	320000	422377	
	FD FOR 5 YEAR	300000	424433	
12	RETIREMENT PARTY/ EXIGENCIES	110000		
	HOUSE-HOLD EXPENSES			
1	FOR THE YEAR 2022 (1.4.22 to 31.3.23)			
	(from savings a/c at Sl. No. 10)			
	Monthly expenses @ 66,666/- pm		800000	
	For Vacation abroad Rs.2,00.000/-		200000	
2	From 1.4.23 to 31.3.2028			
	from PMVVY Scheme(Sl.1 &2) Rs.2,22,000			

Wealth & Wellbeing

	from SCSS Scheme (Sl.3 & 4) Rs.2,22,000			
	from GOI Bonds (Sl.5 &6) Rs.1,43,000			
	From FDs (Sl. 11) Rs.4,18,000			
	Monthly expenses @ 67,000/- pm and			
	For vacations abroad 2,00,000/- every year			
	From 1.4.28 to 31.3.2042			
	from PMVVY Scheme(Sl.1 & 2) Rs.2,22,000*			
	from SCSS Scheme (Sl.3 & 4) Rs.2,22,000*			
	from GOI Bonds (Sl.5 & 6) Rs.1,43,000*			
	from PPF A/C Rs.7,50,000		1337000	
	*Assuming re-investment in same/similar schemes			
	Monthly expenses @ Rs. 80,000/- p.m.			
	Vacations abroad Rs.2,27,000			
	PPF Deposit Rs.1,50,000			
	At 81 years of age, you will still be having			
	approx. Rs.1.10 Crores to live CASH RICH			
	till you are alive & leave balance for kids.			
	(Rs.29 lac PMVVY+Rs.30 lac SCSS+Rs.20 lac GOI Bonds + 21 lacs MF + 10 lacs PPF)			
	IT IS POWER OF COMPOUNDING}			

| PPF DEPOSIT Mr. Mukherjee (FOR NEXT 20 YEARS) |||||||
Op. Bal.	Intt. Rate	Cl.bal.	Interest	Withdrawal	Annual Dep. (Before 5th Apr)	Year
3000000	0.071	3213000	213000	0	150000	Apr-22
3363000	0.071	3601772	238773		150000	Apr-23
3751772	0.071	4018148	266376		150000	Apr-24
4168148	0.071	4464086	295938		150000	Apr-25
4614086	0.071	4941686	327600		150000	Apr-26
5091686	0.071	5453195	361509		150000	Apr-27
5603195	0.071	6001022	397826	750000	150000	Apr-28
5401022	0.071	5784494	383472	750000	150000	Apr-29
5184494	0.071	5552592	368099	750000	150000	Apr-30
4952592	0.071	5304226	351634	750000	150000	Apr-31
4704226	0.071	5038226	334000	750000	150000	Apr-32
4438226	0.071	4753339	315114	750000	150000	Apr-33
4153339	0.071	4448226	294887	750000	150000	Apr-34
3848226	0.071	4121450	273224	750000	150000	Apr-35
3521450	0.071	3771472	250023	750000	150000	Apr-36
3171472	0.071	3396647	225174	750000	150000	Apr-37
2796647	0.071	2995208	198562	750000	150000	Apr-38
2395208	0.071	2565268	170060	750000	150000	Apr-39
1965268	0.071	2104802	139534	750000	150000	Apr-40
1504802	0.071	1611643	106841	750000	150000	Apr-41
1011643	0.071	1083469	71827			Apr-42

Wealth & Wellbeing

ILLUSTRATION – 8

Mr. Nirmal is retiring on 31st March 2022 on attaining the age of 60 years. He is under stress as he has liabilities on his head. His son is doing MBA and his last semester fees of Rs.5 lakh have to be paid in September 2022. His daughter has completed her engineering studies last year only and now working in a reputed IT firm. Parents are planning to marry her after two years and they expect an estimated expenditure of Rs.10 lakh to be kept from retirement funds for her marriage besides using the daughter's income. Mr. Nirmal has spent a good amount on the studies of his children and is now left with a total retirement corpus of Rs.8 lacs only besides a balance of Rs.12 lacs in his PPF account and Rs.7 lakh in his wife's PPF Account.

His monthly estimated expenditure is Rs. 45,000-50,000/- per month including exigencies and he wishes to spend Rs.50,000/- every year on pilgrimage/vacation.

Tentative Retirement financial planning for Mr. Nirmal will be as under:-

SL.NO.	PARTICULARS	INVESTMENT	MATURITY AMOUNT	PERIOD
I	RETIREMENT PROCEEDS 1.4.2022	8300000		
II	LIABILITIES:			
	Son's education			
	FD for 6 months	485000	502124	
	Daughter's marriage			
	FD for 2 years	900000	1033994	
III	INVESTMENTS:			
1	PMVVY SCHEME (LIC)	1450000		
	You will get Rs.1,11,000/- every year for 10 yrs		111000 p.a.	From Apr.23
2	PO-SENIOR CITIZEN SAVINGS SCHEME	1500000	111000 p.a.	for 8 years
	Deposit for 5 years			

Steps To Retirement Planning & Illustrations

	Income Rs.27,750/- per quarter			
	(Please extend for 3 years after maturity)			
	(Thereafter make FD of this amount)			
3	DEPOSIT IN PPF A/C (APR.22) - SELF	150000		
4	DEPOSIT IN PPF A/C (APR.22) - WIFE	150000		
5	FDs for DEPOSIT IN PPF A/C - SELF			
	FD FOR 1 YEAR (MAT. 2nd April)	140000	150060	
	FD FOR 2 YEAR (MAT. 2nd April)	135000	155099	
	FD FOR 3 YEAR (MAT. 2nd April)	125000	153930	
	FD FOR 4 YEAR (MAT. 2nd April)	115000	151792	
	FD FOR 5 YEAR (MAT. 2nd April)	110000	155626	
	(Intt. @ 7% p.a. considered)			
6	FDs for DEPOSIT IN PPF A/C - WIFE			
	FD FOR 1 YEAR (MAT. 2nd April)	140000	150060	
	FD FOR 2 YEAR (MAT. 2nd April)	135000	155099	
	FD FOR 3 YEAR (MAT. 2nd April)	125000	153930	
	FD FOR 4 YEAR (MAT. 2nd April)	115000	151792	
	FD FOR 5 YEAR (MAT. 2nd April)	110000	155626	
7	BALANCE IN SAVINGS A/C	600000		
	(FLEXI ACCOUNT OF SBI)			
8	FDs for HOUSEHOLD EXPENSES			

Wealth & Wellbeing

8.1	FD FOR 1 YEAR (MAT. 2nd April)	405000	434103	
8.2	FD FOR 2 YEAR (MAT. 2nd April)	380000	436575	
8.3	FD FOR 3 YEAR (MAT. 2nd April)	355000	437161	
8.4	FD FOR 4 YEAR (MAT. 2nd April)	335000	442176	
8.5	FD FOR 5 YEAR (MAT. 2nd April)	315000	445655	
	(Intt. @ 7% p.a. considered)			
9	RETIREMENT PARTY	25000		
	HOUSE-HOLD EXPENSES			
1	FOR THE YEAR 2022		650000	
	(from savings a/c at Sl. No. 7)			
	Monthly expenses @ Rs.50,000/- p.m.			
	For Travel/Vacations - Rs.50,000/- p.a.			
2	From 1.4.23 to 31.3.2028			
	from PMVVY Scheme Rs.1,11,000			
	from SCSS Scheme Rs.1,11,000			
	from FD at Sl. 8 Rs.4,35,000		657000	
	(Avg. taken for Sl. No. 8.1 to 8.5)			
	Monthly Expenses @ Rs.54,750/- p.m.			
3	From 1.4.28 onwards			
	from PMVVY Scheme* Rs.1,11,000			
	from SCSS Scheme* Rs.1,11,000			
	From PPF A/c. - self Rs.3,00,000**			

Steps To Retirement Planning & Illustrations

	From PPF A/c. - wife Rs.2,00,000**		722000#		
	* assuming re-investing in same such scheme				
	** Rs.1,50,000/- kept for deposit in PPF (Till 80 yrs) # Extra amount will take care of inflation				
4	At 81 years of age, you will be left with				
	Rs.48,50 lacs approx (14.50 PMVVY+15 SCSS+19 PPF)				

PPF ACCOUNT OF MR. NIRMAL FOR NEXT 20 YEARS						
Op. Bal.	Intt. Rate	Cl.bal.	Interest	Withdrawal	Annual Dep. (Before 5th Apr)	Year
700000	0.071	749700	49700	0	150000	Apr-22
899700	0.071	963579	63879		150000	Apr-23
1113579	0.071	1192643	79064		150000	Apr-24
1342643	0.071	1437970	95328		150000	Apr-25
1587970	0.071	1700716	112746		150000	Apr-26
1850716	0.071	1982116	131401		150000	Apr-27
2132116	0.071	2283497	151380	350000	150000	Apr-28
2083497	0.071	2231425	147928	350000	150000	Apr-29
2031425	0.071	2175656	144231	350000	150000	Apr-30
1975656	0.071	2115927	140271	350000	150000	Apr-31
1915927	0.071	2051958	136031	350000	150000	Apr-32
1851958	0.071	1983447	131489	350000	150000	Apr-33
1783447	0.071	1910071	126625	350000	150000	Apr-34
1710071	0.071	1831486	121415	350000	150000	Apr-35
1631486	0.071	1747321	115835	350000	150000	Apr-36
1547321	0.071	1657181	109860	350000	150000	Apr-37
1457181	0.071	1560641	103460	350000	150000	Apr-38
1360641	0.071	1457246	96605	350000	150000	Apr-39
1257246	0.071	1346511	89264	350000	150000	Apr-40
1146511	0.071	1227913	81402	350000	150000	Apr-41
1027913	0.071	1100894	72982			Apr-42

ILLUSTRATION – 9

Mr. Ghosh is superannuating from a senior post in PSE on 31st March 2022. His only son is well settled abroad and has no intention to come back to India. He has purchased a beautiful flat around 10 years back in his hometown and wishes to settle there after retirement with his wife who is also a senior citizen. They do not have any liability. Mr. Ghosh is worried about investing his total retirement corpus of Rs.1.80 crores and wishes to invest his hard-earned money safely as he is averse to risk-taking and is therefore looking for safer investments only. He opened a PPF account around 14 years back and there is a balance of Rs.25 lacs in his PPF account.

Mr. Ghosh has estimated his monthly expenditure which will be around Rs.80,000/- p.m. including payment of taxes, etc. He also wishes to travel every year i.e. one year within the country and one year abroad and has estimated that he will be requiring Rs.1 lakh every alternate year for within-country travel and around Rs. 2 lakh every alternate year for travel abroad for the next 10 years. He further wishes to visit his son immediately after retirement and spend some time with him for which he has estimated an expenditure of Rs. 2 lakh.

Tentative Retirement financial planning for Mr. Ghosh will be as under:-

SL.NO.	PARTICULARS	INVESTMENT	MATURITY AMOUNT	PERIOD
I	RETIREMENT PROCEEDS 1.4.2022	18000000		
II	INVESTMENTS:			
1	PMVVY SCHEME (LIC) - SELF	1450000		
	You will get Rs.1,11,000/- every year for 10 years		111000 p.a.	From Apr.23
2	PMVVY SCHEME (LIC) - WIFE	1450000		

Steps To Retirement Planning & Illustrations

	You will get Rs.1,11,000/- every year for 10 years		111000 p.a.	From Apr.23
3	PO-SENIOR CITIZEN SAVINGS SCHEME-SELF	1500000	111000 p.a.	for 8 years
	(Extend for 3 years & thereafter re-invest)			
4	PO-SENIOR CITIZEN SAVINGS SCHEME-WIFE	1500000	111000 p.a.	for 8 years
	(Extend for 3 years & thereafter re-invest)			
5	GOI (TAXABLE) BONDS-2020 - self	1000000	71500 p.a.	for 7 years
6	GOI (TAXABLE) BONDS-2020 - wife	1000000	71500 p.a.	for 7 years
7	PO MIS (JOINT NAME)	900000		
	(open RD for 5 years for monthly interest)		345000	after 5 yrs
	(keep re-investing to beat inflation)			
7	PPF ACCOUNT (APRIL 2022)	150000		
8	FD FOR PPF DEPOSITS (NEXT 5 YEARS)			
	FD FOR 1 YEAR	140000	150060	
	FD FOR 2 YEAR	135000	155099	
	FD FOR 3 YEAR	125000	153930	
	FD FOR 4 YEAR	115000	151792	
	FD FOR 5 YEAR	110000	155626	
9	MUTUAL FUNDS (DEBT/INDEX) - SELF	1000000		
10	MUTUAL FUNDS (DEBT/INDEX) - WIFE	1000000		
11	EXIGENCIES/ EMERGENCIES			
11.1	5 YEARS FD IN SMALL FINANCE BANK 1	350000	507482	after 5 yrs
	(open a/c in your name)			

Wealth & Wellbeing

11.2	5 YEARS FD IN SMALL FINANCE BANK 1	350000	507482	after 5 yrs
	(open a/c in spouse name)			
	(interest @ 7.5% considered (prevailing rate)			
11.3	5 YEARS FD IN SMALL FINANCE BANK 2	350000	507482	after 5 yrs
	(open a/c in your name)			
11.4	5 YEARS FD IN SMALL FINANCE BANK 2	350000	507482	after 5 yrs
	(open a/c in spouse name)			
	(interest @ 7.5% considered (prevailing rate)			
11.5	NSC 8th ISSUE - SELF	250000	347373	after 5 yrs
11.6	NSC 8th ISSUE - WIFE	250000	347373	
11.7	KVP	200000	400000	after 10 yrs+
11.8	KVP	200000	400000	
12	FOR TOUR-TRAVEL - 10 years			
	(Rs.1 lac alternate year for within country)			
	(Rs.2 lac alternate year for travel abroad)			
	FD for 1 year	100000	107186	
	FD for 2 years	180000	206799	
	FD for 3 years	85000	104672	
	FD for 4 years	155000	204589	
	FD for 5 years	75000	106108	
	FD for 6 years	140000	212302	
	FD for 7 years	70000	113779	
	FD for 8 years	125000	217777	
	FD for 9 years	60000	112044	
	FD for 10 years	110000	220176	

13	IN SAVINGS A/C (for first year expenses)			
	(open a flexi savings a/c)	1200000		
14	FD For HOUSEHOLD EXPENSES			
	FD FOR 1 YEAR	400000	428744	
	FD FOR 2 YEARS	370000	425086	
	FD FOR 3 YEARS	350000	431004	
	FD FOR 4 YEARS	330000	435577	
	FD FOR 5 YEARS	310000	438581	
15	RETIREMENT PARTY	65000		
	HOUSE-HOLD EXPENSES			
1	FOR THE YEAR 2022 (1.4.22 to 31.3.23)			
	(from savings a/c at Sl. No. 13)			
	Monthly expenses @ 80,000/- pm		1000000	
	For Visiting his son abroad Rs.2,00.000/-		200000	
2	From 1.4.23 to 31.3.2028			
	from PMVVY Scheme(Sl.1 &2) Rs.2,22,000			
	from SCSS Scheme (Sl.3 & 4) Rs.2,22,000			
	from GOI Bonds (Sl.5 & 6) Rs.1,43,000			
	From FDs (Sl. 14) Rs.4,25,000		1012000 p.a.	
	Monthly expenses @ 80,000/- pm			
3	From 1.4.28 to 31.3.2042			
	from PMVVY Scheme(Sl.1 &2) Rs.2,22,000*			
	from SCSS Scheme (Sl.3 & 4) Rs.2,22,000*			

	from GOI Bonds (Sl.5 & 6) Rs.1,43,000*			
	from PPF A/C Rs.6,60,000		1247000 p.a	
	*Assuming re-investment in same/similar schemes			
	Monthly expenses Rs. 91,400/- pm			
	PPF Deposit Rs.1,50,000			
	(After 5 years, you will get Rs.3.45 lakh from MIS/RD)			

At 81 years of age, you will still be having approximately Rs. 1.75 crores with you.

You have invested Rs. 1.80 crores and left with balance of Rs.1.75 crores after spending a CASH-RICH life of your choice for 20 years, it is "POWER OF COMPOUNDING".

PPF DEPOSIT Mr. Ghosh (FOR NEXT 20 YEARS)

Op. Bal.	Intt. Rate	Cl.bal.	Interest	Withdrawal	Annual Dep. (Before 5th Apr)	Year
2500000	0.071	2677500	177500	0	150000	Apr-22
2827500	0.071	3028252	200752		150000	Apr-23
3178252	0.071	3403908	225656		150000	Apr-24
3553908	0.071	3806235	252327		150000	Apr-25
3956235	0.071	4237127	280892		150000	Apr-26
4387127	0.071	4698613	311486		150000	Apr-27
4848613	0.071	5192864	344251	660000	150000	Apr-28
4682864	0.071	5015347	332483	660000	150000	Apr-29
4505347	0.071	4825226	319879	660000	150000	Apr-30
4315226	0.071	4621607	306381	660000	150000	Apr-31
4111607	0.071	4403531	291924	660000	150000	Apr-32
3893531	0.071	4169971	276440	660000	150000	Apr-33
3659971	0.071	3919829	259858	660000	150000	Apr-34
3409829	0.071	3651926	242098	660000	150000	Apr-35
3141926	0.071	3365003	223077	660000	150000	Apr-36
2855003	0.071	3057708	202705	660000	150000	Apr-37
2547708	0.071	2728595	180887	660000	150000	Apr-38
2218595	0.071	2376115	157520	660000	150000	Apr-39
1866115	0.071	1998609	132494	660000	150000	Apr-40
1488609	0.071	1594300	105691	660000	150000	Apr-41
1084300	0.071	1161285	withdraw & enjoy			Apr-42

Wealth & Wellbeing

ILLUSTRATION – 10

Let's assume Mr. Ramprasad is going to retire on 30TH April 2022 on attaining the age of 60 years. He has a total retirement corpus of Rs.180 lacs including maturity of LIC policy and his savings plus balance of Rs. 5 lacs in his PPF Account. He will get pension of Rs.3,660/- from EPFO.

He has to spend around Rs.22,00,000/- on construction of first floor of his house immediately after retirement as he wish to settle in his home with parents. He has to pay fee of Rs.5,00,000/- for his daughter's PG studies in May 2023. He has planned marriage of his daughter in December 2026 for which he has estimated an expenditure of Rs. 15 lacs. He has estimated house-hold expenditure of Rs.60,000/- per month after retirement.

Tentative Retirement financial planning for Mr. Ramprasad will be as under:-

SL.NO.	PARTICULARS	INVESTMENT	MATURITY AMOUNT	PERIOD
I	RETIREMENT PROCEEDS (1st May 2022)		18000000	
	Liabilities:			
i	Construction of 1st Floor	2200000		Jun-22
ii	Daughter's PG Studies			
	FD for 1 year - 1st May 2022	475000	500000	May-23
iii	Daughter's Marriage			
	FD for 3.5 years in Jana Bank (self+wife)*	400000	519700	Dec.26
	FD for 3.5 years in Jana Bank (wife+self)	400000	519700	Dec.26
	*Account in the name of self+wife & wife+ Self			
	are separately insured. Intt. @ 7.55%			

Steps To Retirement Planning & Illustrations

	FD for 990 DAYS in Ujjivan Bank (self+wife)	410000	503553	Oct.26
	(Interest @ 7.65%)			
	INVESTMENTS:			
1	PO-SENIOR CITIZEN SAVINGS SCHEME	1500000		
	Deposit for 5 years			
	Income Rs.27,750/- per quarter			27,750/- per qtr.
	(Please open for another 5 years)			
2	LIC SCHEME (PMVVY Yojana)	1450000		From June 23
	Rs.1,11,000/- every year for 10 years			
3	PO - MONTHLY INCOME SCHEME	900000		
	900000 in joint name			
	(Open RD A/C with PO for Rs.5000/-			
	maturity proceeds 900000 + 3,48,484/-			
	Open fresh MIS for 9 lacs and use INTEREST EARNED for beating inflation (re-invest 3 times)			
	(You can keep money in autosweep a/c of yr bank)			
4	FDs FOR DEPOSIT IN PPF A/C. FOR NEXT 20 yrs)-SELF			
	CUM. FD FOR 1 YEAR#	145000		153292
	CUM.FD FOR 2 YEARS#	135000		151180
	CUM FD FOR 3 YEARS#	130000		155201
	CUM FD FOR 4 YEARS#	120000		151978
	NSC (5 YEARS)	110000		152844

Wealth & Wellbeing

	NSC (5 YEARS)*	470000		653062
	*Convert into 5 fds/nsc as above)			
	KVP**	550000		1100000
	** convert into 5 fds/nsc as above)			
	#current SBI FD rates taken for calculations			
5	GOI FLEXI RATE BONDS	1000000		35,750/- half yly
6	GOI FLEXI RATE BONDS	1000000		35,750/- half yly
	(for 7 years @ 7.15% payable half yearly)			
7	**FOR EMERGENCY/ EXIGENCIES**			
	NSC 5 YEARS	500000		694746
	KVP 10 YRS 4 MONTHS	300000		600000
	FD for 990 days (wife+self) in Ujjivan Bank@7.65%	400000		491271
8	**INVESTMENT IN MUTUAL FUNDS**			
	EQUITY FUNDS	500000		
	INDEX FUNDS	500000		
	DEBT FUNDS	500000		
	(Please take advice of Consultant before investing)			
9	**FD FOR HOUSEHOLD EXPENSES**			
	FOR 1 YEAR	365000		385873
	FOR 2 YEAR	345000		386348
	FOR 3 YEAR	330000		393971
	FOR 4 YEAR	310000		392611
	FOR 5 YEAR	290000		393608
	FOR 6 YEAR	270000		389550
	FOR 7 YEAR	260000		398755
	FOR 8 YEAR	250000		407574

	FOR 9 YEAR	240000		415921
	FOR 10 YEARS	230000		423702
	KVP for 10 yrs 4 months (for 11TH YEAR)	225000		450000
10	KEEP IN SAVINGS A/C FOR 1 ST YEAR EXPENSES	750000		
	(preferably in SBI Flexi account)			
11	Retirement Party	40000		
	HOUSE HOLD EXPENSES			
1	From May 22 to April 23			
	From Sl. No. 10 @ Rs.62,500/- pm			
2	From May 23 to April 33			
	EPFO Pension Rs. 43,920			
	From SCSS (Sl. No. 1) Rs.1,11,000			
	From PMVVY (Sl. No. 2) Rs.1,11,000			
	From Bonds (Sl. No. 5&6) Rs.1,43,000			
	From FD at Sl. No. 9 Rs.3,85,000		793920	
	Monthly Expenses @ Rs.66,000/- per month+ Interest earned on MIS+ Income from MFs			
3	From May 33 onwards			
	EPFO Pension Rs. 43,920			
	From SCSS (Sl. No. 1) Rs.1,11,000*			
	From PMVVY (Sl. No. 2) Rs.1,11,000*			
	From Bonds (Sl. No. 5&6) Rs.1,43,000*			
	From PPF A/c (enclosed) Rs.5,50,000**		958920	

Wealth & Wellbeing

	*Assuming re-investment in same/similar scheme **For deposit in PPF a/c Rs.1,50,000/- p.a.			
	Monthly Expenses @ Rs.67,400/- pm + interest Earned on MIS+Income from MFs			
	At the Age of 81, you will still have			
	about 100 lacs to enjoy or leave for daughter			

| PPF Account of Mr. Ramprasad for next 20 years |||||||
Op. Bal.	Intt. Rate	Cl.bal.	Interest	Withdrawal	Annual Dep. (Before 5th Apr)	Year
472001	0.071	506616	34615	0	150000	Apr-24
656616	0.071	704769	48154	0	150000	Apr-25
854769	0.071	917455	62686	0	150000	Apr-26
1067455	0.071	1145738	78283	0	150000	Apr-27
1295738	0.071	1390763	95025	0	150000	Apr-28
1540763	0.071	1653757	112994	0	150000	Apr-29
1803757	0.071	1936038	132281	0	150000	Apr-30
2086038	0.071	2239020	152982	0	150000	Apr-31
2389020	0.071	2564222	175202	0	150000	Apr-32
2714222	0.071	2913273	199051	0	150000	Apr-33
3063273	0.071	3287922	224649	550000	150000	Apr-34
2887922	0.071	3099712	211790	550000	150000	Apr-35
2699712	0.071	2897699	197987	550000	150000	Apr-36
2497699	0.071	2680871	183172	550000	150000	Apr-37
2280871	0.071	2448141	167271	550000	150000	Apr-38
2048141	0.071	2198344	150203	550000	150000	Apr-39
1798344	0.071	1930228	131884	550000	150000	Apr-40
1530228	0.071	1642450	112221	550000	150000	Apr-41
1242450	0.071	1333566	91117	550000	150000	Apr-42
933566			withdraw & enjoy			Apr-43

32.
RETIREMENT SATISFACTION GUIDE

Retirement is a major life-changing event like marriage and the psychological process of retirement follows a pattern similar in nature to the emotional phases accompanying marriage.

During the working years, retirement can appear to be both an oncoming burden and also a distant paradise. Although we save for it but often give little thought to what we will do once we reach the goal.

By far the shortest stage in the retirement process is the actual cessation of employment itself. Retirement is often marked by some sort of party or celebration and this event can be compared to the ceremony that marks the beginning of a marriage.

Once the retirement celebrations are over, a period often follows where retirees get to do all the things that they wanted to do once they stopped working e.g. travel, hobbies, visiting relatives, etc? However, this phase has no set time frame and will vary depending upon how much honeymoon activity you have planned.

The next phase will be disenchantment which parallels the stage in marriage when the emotional high of the wedding has worn off and the couple now has to get down to the business of building a working relationship together. Retirement isn't a permanent vacation after all; it also brings loneliness, boredom, feelings of uselessness, or disillusionment.

Fortunately, the letdown phase of retirement doesn't last forever. The next phase of reorientation comes where retirees start building a new identity by familiarizing themselves with the landscape of their new circumstances and navigating their lives accordingly. This, however, is the most difficult stage in the emotional retirement process and will take both time and conscious effort to accomplish.

It's time to create a plan; a roadmap for what you want your life to be. We have discussed the financial plan in detail in this book but do you have a plan for how you wish to live the next twenty to thirty years of your life? You can't leave your second innings to chance and hope that you won't be disappointed? Therefore, you must begin exploring how you wish to live your retired life?

Following three insurances are required to ensure healthy, wealthy, and happy retired life:

- Medical Insurance
- Financial Insurance
- Emotional Insurance

We have discussed the first two i.e. take care of your medical needs by taking sufficient Mediclaim policy that must be adequate to meet your requirements depending upon your health condition but doesn't overdo it. If required, consider taking a super-top-up policy to mitigate the medical emergency, if any.

It is impossible to stay happy and healthy without ensuring that you have sufficient money to take care of your second innings till you are alive. Without proper financial planning, you will always live under tension and may invite many physical ailments also. By way of various illustrations in the book, we have seen that if planned properly, we don't need a very big 'retirement corpus'. However, proper budgeting and planning are required to invest the money we have saved for our retired life.

Now comes the most important part of 'retirement' i.e. Emotional Insurance. Please follow the under-mentioned steps to ensure your emotional well-being:-

i) Try to reconnect with your dreams for more practical considerations, or dream about what you want in your life for the first time.
ii) Life is about change and everything changes and we have little or no control over all life's changes. However, we have total

control over what we choose to notice, validate, accentuate. It is therefore important to change your mind.

iii) Begin now training your thoughts to focus on what is 'right' about your life and try to welcome changes.

iv) Commit to being happy. Always remind yourself of the 90/10 principle of Stephen Covey:
"Ten percent of life is made up of what happens to you. Ninety percent of life is decided by how you react". We have no control over 10 percent of what happens to us.

v) To live your second adulthood with freedom, purpose, and passion, stop and look at yourself as well as your physical, emotional and spiritual environment.

vi) Don't leave the important things to chance. Make a plan and get started – one step at a time.

vii) It's time to replace the network of friends and colleagues you enjoy through work. Try to connect with neighbors, relatives, and friends whom you could not contact much due to pre-occupations or paucity of time. Socialization is a key to satisfying retired life.

viii) If you find the thought of retirement stressful or need assistance establishing a road map to reach your goals, consider having discussions with others who have successfully made the transition. However, the following tips may be of great help:

❖ **Keep Working**
The good news is, we're generally staying healthier and more active longer, which means we can work longer. It will also give your portfolio the chance to continue increasing in value for a few more years.

❖ **The budget on the back end**
Create a budget you can stick to just before you retire. Sticking to a budget will help keep you from outliving your nest egg. The idea is not to live frugally for the rest of your life, just wisely.

❖ **Manage your mortgage:**
Avoid the temptation of taking out a second loan or overspending through credit cards to consolidate your debt, buy a new home/car, un-wanted items, etc.

- ❖ **Diversify, Diversify, Diversify**
  The saying, "Don't put all of your eggs in one basket," couldn't apply more to saving for retirement. Try to avoid high-risk investments.

- ❖ **Get in the savings mindset**
  We have understood the 'power of compounding' in the previous chapters. It is therefore essential that you should designate an amount of your pre-tax income to contribute to your retirement savings monthly just like your taxes that will surely help you to make a healthy 'retirement corpus'.

- ❖ **Do nominate but don't handover**
  You have always tried to give by fulfilling the needs of family and children. At this stage of life, it will be very difficult to ask for anything even from your children. Therefore, do nominate, make your 'will' but keep your 'estate' with you only till you are alive.

- ❖ Please remember, happy and peaceful life depends on your 'state of mind' i.e. your attitude towards life.

> *"Your living is determined not so much by what life brings to you as by the attitude you bring to life; not so much by what happens to you as by the way, your mind looks at what happens"*
>
> *-Khalil Gibran*

33.
WILL AND NOMINATION

Many people think that only the very wealthy persons or those with complicated assets need Wills. However, there are many reasons to write a will such as:

- If you don't want to see your family members fighting for your wealth after you.
- You can be clear about who gets what and how much?
- You can keep your assets out of the hands of people you don't want to have (e.g. your estranged relative)
- Your heirs will have a faster and easier time getting access to your assets.

A will is a legal document that sets forth your wishes regarding the distribution of your 'estate'. If you die without a will, those wishes may not be carried out. Further, your heirs may end up spending additional time, money and will be under emotional stress to settle your affairs after you're gone.

'Estate' means all the property like cash, jewelry, house/flats, all investments and savings accounts, etc.

The biggest confusion arise when you think that why I need the will when I have appointed nominees in all my Bank Accounts, FDs, Shares, Insurance Policies, PPF, MFs, etc?

Nomination and Will are two important terms associated with Estate Planning. The process of Estate Planning includes:

- Deciding who all will receive the share of your estate.
- Deciding how and when the beneficiaries will receive their inheritance

- Deciding who will manage the estate.

Nomination:

Nomination is the process of appointing a person to take care of your assets in the event of your death. A nominee could be a family member or a friend or any other person whom you trust. The nomination makes the process of transferring your investments to your nominee smoother. Some investments also allow you to have multiple nominees where you can assign percentages of your money to each one of them and if you don't specify percentages, it is shared equally. Though the nominee is an important person, he/she has no rights over the money or assets unless that is specified under the Will i.e. he is only a custodian of the assets.

In absence of nomination, the process of settling a death claim may require a host of documents, including death succession certificates, a will, or a court order. Although it may sound simple on paper, it ends up being a long-drawn process in real life and it is not a situation in which you would want to put your loved ones at a time, which would anyways be an already emotionally painful situation for them.

Please keep in mind the following points while doing nomination:

- Mention the full name, age, address, and relationship with the nominee.
- Do not write the nomination in favor of "wife" and "children" as a class. Give their specific names and particulars existing at that moment.
- If the nominee is a minor, appoint a person who is a major as an appointee giving his full name, age, address, and relationship to the nominee.
- Keep regularizing "nomination" in all your financial instruments, assets, bank accounts, etc. from time to time.

Will:

Under the Indian Succession Act, 1925 a will has been defined as under:
"A will is the legal declaration of the intention of the testator, concerning his property which he desires to be carried out into effect after his death".

Testator means one who makes and executes the last will. E.g. If Radhika has a will drafted and she executes the will, then Radhika is referred to as the Testator.

A will is a way of succession planning that ensures that the individual's property or any other asset is given to the preferred family members without any dispute at the time of property distribution. Having a will gives you a legal right and an assurance to distribute your property.

The will of the testator must be written by people with sound and clear mind means any person under a state of intoxication, illness or any similar cause cannot make a will i.e. he must be 'mentally capable' and 18 years or older.

There is no legal requirement to register a will. It doesn't even have to be on a stamp paper or notarized. An unregistered will is valid if it conforms to the legal requirement of two witnesses who have signed the will in the presence of the testator and the testator has signed the will in their presence.

Registration of a will simply means that the maker of the will and the witnesses have appeared before the registering authorities and that their identity has been verified.

A will is invalid if it is not properly witnessed or signed. Most commonly, two witnesses must sign the will in the testator's presence after watching the testator sign the will. The witnesses need to be of a certain age, and should generally not stand to inherit anything from the will. Since a will can be written on a blank paper, the signature is the only authentic detail in it. Therefore, the most important aspect of a will is the valid signature of the person making it.

A will can be hand-written or typed. It is to be written specifying one's details, family details, bequeath details, and details of both witnesses. One must make sure that his/her Will is created when one is mentally sound, without any fear, force, coercion, or undue influence.

How to make a Will?

There is no legal or defined format for writing a Will; however, there is a template, which has been generally used for ages. It's simple, logical, and derives from common sense. It only requires remembering the following points while creating a Will:

1) Declaration

In the first paragraph, declare that you are making this will in your full senses and free from any kind of pressure. You have to mention your name, address, age, etc. at the time of writing the will so that it confirms that you are, in your senses.

2) Details of Property and Documents:

The next step is to provide a list of items and their current values, like house/flat, land, bank accounts and fixed deposits, mutual funds, shares, other investments, etc. owned by you. You must also indicate, where all these documents are stored by you.

3) Details of Ownership:

At the end of the will, you should mention who should own your assets and in what proportion, after you have gone. If you are giving your assets to a minor, make sure you appoint a custodian of your assets till the individual you have selected, reaches adult age.

4) Signing the Will:

In the end, once you complete writing your will, you must sign the will very carefully in presence of two independent witnesses, who have to sign after your signature, certifying that you have signed the will in their presence. The date and place also must be indicated clearly at the bottom of the will. Also, make sure that you and the witnesses sign all the pages of the will. The witnesses can be your friends, neighbors, or your colleagues and not the direct beneficiaries in the will.

Keep the Will in an envelope properly sealed after completing all the formalities and the seal must bear your signature and the date of sealing. However, the witnesses need not sign on the seal of the envelope. Keep the Will in a safe place in your home, bank locker, or with a trusted relative. Make sure a beneficiary or the executor knows the location of the will and how to access it.

When a person dies without having made a Will, he is said to have died intestate. In this case, his property is then inherited by his legal heirs following the law of inheritance applicable to him as per his religion.

34.
STEPS TO CHOOSE HAPPINESS

It is often said that money can buy anything but 'happiness'. Many people tend to disagree with this statement as money can buy all the pleasures available on the earth e.g. a big house, big car, lots of servants, costly clothes, accessories, etc., etc. and the list is endless. When all these pleasures give us enjoyment and make us happy then why conclude that money can't buy happiness. It is because these pleasures though give us happiness but it is temporary and these pleasures may keep us happy for some time only. Let me explain with an example.

After I retired from PSE, I joined a company as a Consultant and I was assisting the owner of the company in his marketing efforts. My owner had recently constructed a beautiful house and spent around Rs.20 crores. He was always telling me with a sparkle in his eyes that he got the marble from this place, accessories from that place, and also about many imported items used in his house. His happiness while telling all these things was visible on his face. One day one of our big clients asked us for a meeting at his residence as he was not well. We immediately agreed to meet him at his residence on the appointed date and time as we were expecting a big order from him.

We reached his place on appointed time and at the gate, the security guard enquired about our purpose of visit. On telling him about our meeting, he checked on the intercom and politely asked us to follow him so that he can escort us up to the designated place. When we asked about our car, he asked, don't worry sir, we will park it safely.

The house of our client was awesome and after the meeting, he offered us to look at his newly built house. He showed us the full house with a big smile on his face and told us that he has constructed this house recently by spending around Rs.35 Crores. He was telling about flooring, ceiling, other fixtures, etc. with pride and wih twinkle in his eyes.

While coming back from the meeting, my owner kept on yelling how proudly the client was telling about his house, flooring, furniture, fixtures, fittings, etc. Somehow I felt from his tone that he was not happy. The question however was, whether he was unhappy because the client was proudly telling about his house or he was unhappy because his house was not as good as his client's was. Incidentally, after that day, we never had discussions about his house which earlier was a regular phenomenon i.e. the 'happiness' after spending Rs. 20 crore is now over.

This may be true for small-small pleasures also as the pleasures which you can buy with money will give you happiness but they will make you happy for some time only whereas true happiness is a feeling that lasts for a long period.

Money can buy you a bed but not the sleep, medicines but not the good health, material possessions but not true love. It is your 'attitude' towards life that will decide your happiness.

True happiness is living a life full of satisfaction, contentment, joy, and peace. Happiness is a state of mind; it is an emotion; it is feeling good from within; therefore no one can make you happy until you decide to be happy.

I always keep on telling that 'pleasure' and 'joy' are not synonyms, 'pleasure' is enjoying the happiness which is either bought or borrowed from others whereas 'joy' is giving happiness to others even at the cost of your time, energy or money.

You help someone in need without expecting anything in return; you will remember it for a long time and whenever you will remember the incident, it will make you happy from within. I daily go to the park in our Apartment with my grandson after his school where he plays with his 8-10 friends. All the kids want me also to play with them. They keep on shouting, laughing, running around with me and the happiness on their faces is visible. Although it is tiring and exhausting for me but the 'joy' of making kids happy gives me immense happiness from within. At times, I give them surprise chocolate, candy, or lollypop party and their sparkling faces make me happy. That's 'joy' of giving for me and 'pleasure' of taking for kids and the result is both are happy i.e. me and the kids.

Now, when we have secured our future by wisely investing our money and sure that we shall be able to sustain our living peacefully till we are alive. Let's try to practice the steps to choose 'happiness'. Though very little depends on your genetics also, happiness is greatly a matter of choice. Therefore, have a burning desire to be happy always and try to follow these 10 simple steps:

1. Always be grateful:
Happy people choose to focus on the positive aspects of life i.e. you were blessed to have a good education, food, shelter, clothing, etc., and your family, friends, and colleagues always supported you whenever in need. There may be many reasons to be grateful for. Try to express your gratitude as and when possible.

2. Keep Smiling:
Many studies have concluded that making an emotion-filled face carries influence over feelings. Try to make a conscious effort to make a smiling face always. You can program yourself to experience happiness by choosing to smile. Further, all the pretty smiles you'll receive in return for flashing yours are also guaranteed to increase your happiness level.

3. Learn to forgive and forget:
Even if you have a complaint towards a person, situation, or yourself, hold it back instead of entering into a verbal argument. Try to keep it to yourself and most likely you will be able to diffuse an unhealthy, unhappy environment. Even, you'll experience the joy of choosing peace in a difficult situation.

4. Practice self-discipline:
Embrace and practice at least one act of self-discipline each day. This could be exercise, budgeting, or guided learning. The choice is yours and largely depends upon what your life needs today to continue growing. Explore the options, find them, practice them and celebrate them.

5. Exploit your Strengths:

Everyone has natural talents, strengths, and abilities and if used effectively, we feel joyous and alive. Embrace your strengths and choose to operate within your giftedness each day, if required, even outside your employment. The joy of using your inherent talents will keep you happy always.

6. Develop good food habits:

Caring for your physical well-being can have significant benefits for your emotional standing as your physical health will positively impact your spiritual and emotional well-being. Always try to eat healthy foods as staying fit will enhance your happiness every day.

7. Be Courteous:

I read in my school book that **"courtesy costs nothing but add charms to life"**. Therefore, try to be courteous and treat everyone you meet with kindness, patience, and grace. Often use these three magic words i.e. sorry, please and thank you, and see the magic of bringing a smile not only on others' faces but yours also. We are here for the "pursuit of happiness".

8. Learn to Meditate:

Studies confirm the importance and life-giving benefits of meditation. Try to take out some time and use meditation to search inward, connect spiritually and improve your happiness. The first step is to sit in silence for some time alone in solitude.

9. Bounce Back:

Life can be difficult at times as nobody escapes without pain. When the times are difficult and you are stuck in misery and sunk in despair, learn to bounce back with the help of two pillars – 'faith' and 'hope'. With the help of these two pillars, you can learn to live a transformed life of joy and most likely you will also develop the ability to comfort others in their pain.

10. Be happy always:

It's your choice to be happy always as happiness is not momentary and not dependent on material possessions. It is a way of life, pulling the happiness triggers e.g. make others happy, react positively, keep counting your blessings, learn to appreciate, etc. and stay away from the negative emotions e.g. anger, jealousy, worry, ego, criticism, etc. Make positive attitude a way of your life and be happy all the time.

> *"Most people are about as happy as they make up their minds to be."*
>
> *-Abraham Lincoln*

www.ingramcontent.com/pod-product-compliance
Lightning Source LLC
Chambersburg PA
CBHW030926180526
43163CD00002B/476